HIGH TECH AND HOT POT

HIGH TECH
and HOT POT

REVEALING ENCOUNTERS INSIDE THE REAL CHINA

STEPHAN ORTH
TRANSLATION BY JAMIE MCINTOSH

GREYSTONE BOOKS
Vancouver/Berkeley

20 21 22 23 24   5 4 3 2 1

Greystone Books Ltd.
greystonebooks.com

Cataloguing data available from Library and Archives Canada
ISBN 978-1-77164-562-1 (pbk.)
ISBN 978-1-77164-564-5 (epub)

Copy editing by Shirarose Wilensky
Proofreading by Alison Strobel
Cover and text design by Fiona Siu
Cover photographs by Stephan Orth and Stefen Chow
Photo credits: © Stephan Orth, except for the photo on page 32
© Stephan Orth/Pitu app; and the photo on page 131 © Stefen Chow.
Map by Birgit Kohlhaas

Printed and bound in Canada on ancient-forest-friendly paper by Friesens

Greystone Books gratefully acknowledges the Musqueam, Squamish and
Tsleil-Waututh peoples on whose land our office is located.

Greystone Books thanks the Canada Council for the Arts, the British
Columbia Arts Council, the Province of British Columbia through
the Book Publishing Tax Credit and the Government of Canada for
supporting our publishing activities.

The translation of this work was supported by a grant from the
Goethe-Institut.

CONTENTS

For Xiao Bai

. . . .

A grandpa and his grandson admire the view from a hill. The grandson says: "The neon lights are pretty because they make the city colorful." The grandpa replies: "Before there were neon lights people could see the stars, which was much prettier."

Write an essay on this subject.

An exercise for teenagers preparing for the gaokao exams for university acceptance in the province of Liaoning

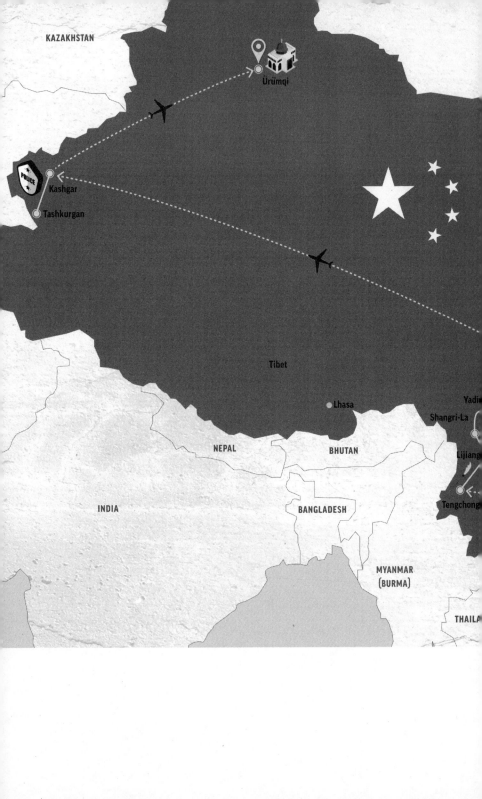

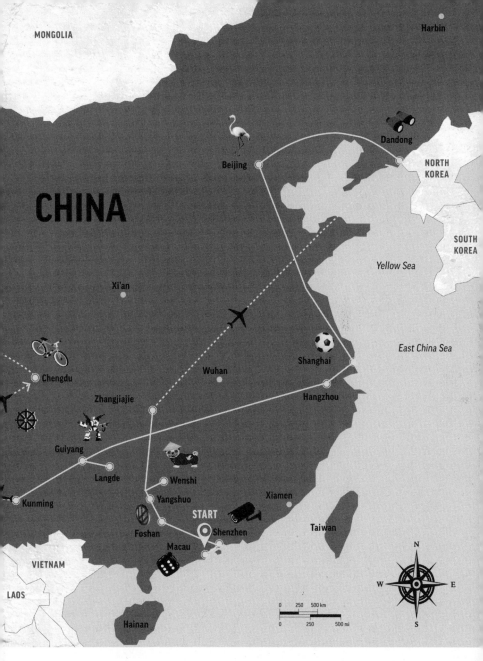

MONGOLIA

Harbin

CHINA

Beijing

Dandong

NORTH
KOREA

SOUTH
KOREA

Yellow Sea

Xi'an

East China Sea

Chengdu

Wuhan

Shanghai

Zhangjiajie

Hangzhou

Guiyang

Langde

Wenshi

Xiamen

Kunming

Yangshuo

START

Taiwan

Foshan

Shenzhen

Macau

VIETNAM

LAOS

Hainan

N

W   E

S

0   250   500 km

0   250   500 mi

12 weeks
Total mileage 9,360 (15,063 km)
BY PLANE: 3,900 (6,276 km)
BY TRAIN: 3,300 (5,311 km)
BY BUS/CAR: 2,120 (3,412 km)
BY SHIP: 40 (64 km)

PREFACE

MY TRIP TO China took place many months before the whole world knew about a city called Wuhan. With 11 million inhabitants, it was one of those megacities that, for a long time, few people outside of China had ever heard of. In January 2020, I was following the events of the burgeoning pandemic from a distance. But since I had been to China recently, the footage of empty streets in huge cities, the thought of people stuck in those high-rise apartments I had visited, stuck for sixty or seventy days without being allowed to set foot outside even once—it all probably felt less far away for me than for people watching the news without firsthand experience of traveling in China.

I was still in contact with some of my friends from the trip and heard about their coronavirus experiences. You will meet some of them in this book—for instance, Qing, a policewoman who works in a prison. Over email, she told me about her new working routines in the time of COVID-19: guards at the prison were divided into three groups. For the first two weeks, Group A stayed at home, and Group B went into quarantine in a separate guards' unit with dorms, which they weren't allowed to leave. Meanwhile, Group C, who had already completed the two-week quarantine, did the actual work in the prison—not going home between shifts, of course. The groups take turns in this rotation, so that every employee spends four weeks isolated from their family and two weeks at home, all to make sure the inmates won't get the virus.

You will also meet the artist Lin, who managed to escape China after I visited her and now lives in another country (I'm quite happy about this, as I felt her eagerness to speak up against the government was going to get her in trouble). Recently, I saw some of her social media posts where she criticized China for holding back important facts about human-to-human transmission of the virus.

Another Chinese friend from Beijing (she is not mentioned in the book) started writing a corona diary on Facebook. She has chronicled her anger about the mistakes in the Chinese response and the government's lack of transparency. On February 1, she wrote about the problem of the lack of supplies in hospitals. On February 3, she posted a photo of a line in front of a restaurant where people stood ten feet apart from each other. Three days later, she posted a photo of a completely empty intersection on a weekday along one of Beijing's busiest roads. Then, on February 11, she advised her readers to "wear a mask and stay healthy," later adding she couldn't believe how slow Western countries were in implementing compulsory masks. Her accounts were like a window into the future and gave me the chance to adapt much more quickly to the changes that became a reality in Europe and North America just a few weeks later. There is something weirdly symbolic about this: my trip to China, the trip you are going to read about, also felt a lot like a look into the future, mainly in terms of high-tech development, surveillance and modern autocratic leadership.

I've always known it is a good thing to travel and learn from the experiences of people in other countries. But only since COVID-19 wreaked havoc around the world have I realized that such knowledge can actually save lives.

STEPHAN ORTH, May 2020

ARRIVING
IN THE FUTURE

I'M RACING THROUGH a labyrinth of skyscrapers made of glass
and concrete in a flying car. The sky is black and the windows
glow coldly; instead of streets, neon light beams show the way.
I hear the sound of a horn—a strange old-fashioned sound—
and react with a lightning-fast maneuver upwards. Just in
time, as I avoid colliding with an approaching flying object that
looks like a cargo train. An LED traffic sign displays some information: October 21, 2052, 9:45, 23 degrees Celsius, rain.

Suddenly, a flying black convertible sports car with a huge
skull decorating the trunk overtakes me. The driver has a human
head with an eye patch and the body of a robot. He brakes right
in front of me and shoots a ray at me from his arm that envel-
ops my passenger, dragging her into his car. She has pink eyes
and hair, and the metallic limbs of a robot's body.

He accelerates and I follow him through the canyons
between the buildings and across a black lake reflecting the

cyan lights of the city. A couple of police jets come to my aid, swishing left and right around me and ramming the bad guy's flying machine. He nose-dives and his passenger tumbles out, but with another lightning-fast maneuver and a plucky hand-grip, I can save her.

Done. The words "winner is human" appear on the screen.

I take off my virtual reality glasses, release my safety belt and stand up. On the way to the exit I have to walk through a store selling plastic swords and zodiac mugs, drones and robots; they even have electric ladybugs and a "baby's first robot." I buy nothing.

Back in the fresh air. "China's First Big-Data Demonstration Park" is written on one poster on the wall of a dark gray building, "Oriental Science Fiction Valley" on another. Both names for the 330-acre complex in Guiyang are somewhat misleading, as what is supposed to be "Oriental" here is not particularly obvious, and "Big-Data" refers not to the massive processing of statistical data but rather the huge computer capacity necessary for creating digital 3-D worlds. Still, there is no harm done if visitors' brains link important futuristic buzzwords to a positive experience.

Carefree young families wander around the site, the children running ahead to other dark gray buildings with attractions called Alien Battlefield, Sky Crisis and Interstellar Lost.

The newly opened park is flooded with visitors, and online comments state that people have to line up for hours on end. Today it doesn't appear so, but maybe it's too early in the day. Staff wear light blue uniforms with silver stripes, a mixture of *Star Trek* chic and tracksuits. On the lapel is a logo of a robot head encompassed by eight rays like a portrayal of a saint.

When they greet visitors, the young men and women raise their right hand in a Spock salute.

A 173-foot-tall sculpture resembling an oversized Transformers action figure dominates the middle of the park. It has colossal feet but a strikingly small head, the same as the one on the uniform lapels, and the body language is that of a commander urging on his army. An army of dozens of smaller statues of cyborgs stand at the edge of a neatly tarred circular path: silent observers with weapons at the ready but at the same time appearing not particularly unfriendly.

I came here to discover how China imagines the future and I find mighty machine gods and humans groomed to uniformity.

A clown twists balloons into cute animal for kids. He doesn't really fit into the science-fiction surroundings, but maybe the park director employed him because he realized that all the gray buildings and robots made the atmosphere a bit grim. If there were an award for the most depressing amusement park in the world, this one would be a front-runner.

A ride called Fly over Guizhou promises light entertainment with a virtual 3-D trip to the top ten sites in Guizhou province: Huangguoshu Waterfall, the Dragon Palace Caves, Hongfeng Lake.

A couple of dozen serpentine metal railings lead to a carriage with room for eight. I am the only passenger. Solitude in China—that's a pretty exclusive experience. The carriage clatters off, but something isn't right. In my digital glasses I can only see a kind of courtyard; the walls around me are light and dark gray like the buildings outside but enclosing me, with no way out. A woman's voice keeps repeating the same Chinese sentence, but I don't understand a single word. I have 360-degree vision, but I can do nothing; I can't make decisions, can't take the initiative.

I take off the virtual reality headset. The raised tracks go in a long curve through a dark, empty hall; on the walls are ducts of a ventilation system. To the left and right is a six-foot drop to the ground, and thirty feet in front of me there seems to be some sort of door. The carriage refuses to move.

Back on with the headset and back to the digital world. Nothing has changed. The walls remain blank; the voice repeats its sentence. I'm quite sure it doesn't say, "Winner is human." I am in a digital no-man's-land, caught in an error of virtual reality.

THE CHINESE DREAM

SIX WEEKS EARLIER

EVERY JOURNEY BEGINS with an idea. In this case it's Yang's idea of printing my face on packages of sausages. "You look trustworthy. With your photo on them, the sales of Chinese sausages will double," she says.

I try imagining such a product on the supermarket shelf. It doesn't really match my professional ambitions, but luckily, she has a few other suggestions.

"You could be a movie star. They are always looking for foreigners for supporting roles. Or go on a dating show. Every woman would want you. You could work as a fake CEO—put on a suit and pretend to be a German manager at trade fairs. Chinese firms will pay you well because they want an international image."

Yang sits on a folding chair in my kitchen in Hamburg, drinking green tea and describing her country as the land of unlimited opportunity. At least for a "long nose" like me.

"English or German teacher—they'll take anyone and pay you three times as much as the locals. Or you could advertise skin-whitening cream."

My Chinese visitor speaks rapidly, almost without taking a breath, as if every tenth of a second of silence is a waste of time. Sometimes a slight twitch in the corner of her mouth betrays a good pinch of humor in her word torrent.

"You could be a fortune-teller with millions of online followers. Grow a beard and people would believe you. Or a rent-a-boyfriend for New Year's parties, to try to calm parents who want their daughters to finally marry. You seem healthy—you could sell a kidney. There's a huge organ market in south China. But be careful they don't steal them from you. As a German, you can always open a bar, a bakery or a butcher shop. It's so unfair. In Europe they only ask me whether I can give massages, but if you go to China, you can be whatever you want. Soon you will be rich and famous."

Yang stumbled across me on Couchsurfing.com, asked for a place to sleep and is now staying on my couch for the weekend. While listening to her monologue, I made up my mind about my next destination. Yang herself hasn't been back home for a few months, because she moved from south China to Berlin to do her master's degree in biology.

"Every day since I've been in Germany I feel a bit more left behind," she says. "I'm becoming lazy."

"What do you mean?"

"In China, everything happens faster. People have goals and begin each new day with pep. In Germany, they wake up and the first thing they think is: *How long is it to the weekend?*"

It's Saturday afternoon and she chats on for hours. Has listless Europe had such an effect on her that she is now capable of such indolence? At the same time, she seems anything but languid; everything about her betrays a certain urgency: her brisk pace, her colorful trainers, even her polo shirt collar, which pokes out from under her sweater on one side while the other side remains tucked in.

"Perhaps the Chinese want to live every day as if it were their last," says Yang. "Work hard because, who knows, maybe tomorrow it will be over?"

"If I knew that today was my last day, I would do a thousand things, but working wouldn't be one of them."

"In China such an attitude is called wasting your youth, squandering the productive years of your life. If you are productive, then you are contributing something to the common good, earning money, or at least doing something for your own benefit. You are not just hanging around and wasting oxygen."

"Sometimes I think wasting oxygen is perfectly okay."

"You lazy *laowai!*" she says, and laughs. *Laowai* means "old foreigner," but another translation is "always a foreigner," which sounds like an indication that China doesn't make life particularly easy for visitors.

· · · · · · · · · ·

I'VE BEEN TO China three times before—in 2008, 2014 and 2017. Everything changes so quickly that each time the country seemed completely different: New skyscraper neighborhoods, new successful companies, new technologies, new codes of behavior. More railway tracks, more airports, more high tech, more restrictions, more people and, in my head each time, a bit more knowledge but also more questions. If this transformation was such an intense experience for me, then what is it like for the Chinese? How do the high-speed changes affect people and their day-to-day lives? And what can we expect when China increasingly influences world affairs in the future?

I want to go there once more, not just because of Yang's promises. I want to try to understand how the Chinese see the world. I want to talk to them about their dreams and fears, about life and love and about where this huge country is heading.

"China has to understand the world better, and the world has to understand China better," said President Xi Jinping in 2016. And it's true there is hardly any other country with a comparable worldwide political influence that has, despite tourism and globalization, remained so unknown to so many.

And a trip to the Middle Kingdom is particularly interesting now because it is going through an epoch-making transformation. After years of incredible economic boom in which clever imitation played a central role, there is now a trend towards creating something of their own, something new. Under the slogan "Made in China 2025," President Xi wants to mold the digital future, banking on artificial intelligence, high tech and a form of surveillance state that makes Orwell's ideas look tame. At the same time, China is buying into businesses worldwide, developing new trade routes with the One Belt, One Road initiative and making whole countries dependent on China by granting credit. All over the world, Western trading partners are losing ground as China secures one major contract after the other. Few have noticed just how large their economic influence already is. While their northern neighbor Russia acts like a bogus giant geopolitically, China behaves like a bogus dwarf, with "hide your strength and bide your time," the motto of previous party leader Deng Xiaoping, proving to be an ingenious strategy. While their rival, the USA, is withdrawing from

8

foreign policy responsibilities and terminating all sorts of alliances according to the slogan "America First," China is ready to refashion the global economy according to its own rules. Certainties, which had seemed steadfast for decades, are beginning to shake. With its economic success, this new world power offers an ideological counter-model to democracy, making Europe or North America appear ineffectual, discordant and slow in comparison.

So, Yang is right, and Xi Jinping, too. In China, everything is happening quicker, and we need to know more about one another.

Once the weekend was over and Yang had left my couch, I downloaded a visa application.

NO BOOK
ABOUT CHINA

CHINA DOESN'T WANT foreign travelers to use hotels other than those that have been specially prescribed for them. China doesn't want visitors staying overnight in private accommodations without registering with the police. China doesn't want foreigners to witness poverty when the official narrative stresses progress. China wants sycophants not questioners, propaganda not realism, honeyed lips not hair in the soup.

And China wants tourists to check out the attractions. But, to me, people who travel just to tick off the top sites are rather like guests meeting Bill Gates, Banksy and Angela Merkel at a pajama party only to say afterwards that the chandelier in the hall was quite pretty. On this trip, China's magnificent showplaces will only play a peripheral role. I want to look behind the facade of the new superpower. I want to enter the living rooms.

On a miserable February morning, I ride to the Elbchaussee, a grand boulevard with the villas of shipping bosses, classical country houses and fancy restaurants. The Chinese consul has invited me for a private chat. Now, is it an honor or a threat?

A visit to a consul—that sounds like wood-paneled walls, heavy leather armchairs and old single malt whiskey. I was way off. The official residence of the Chinese consulate general is, compared to the neighboring houses, pure understatement, more like a village post office than a showcase palace. Plastic chairs, a rack with Chinese newspapers, waiting stacks of forms in plastic folders and the smells of photocopiers, jasmine tea and floor cleaner.

A security guard leads me to a counter in the next room. A clerk sitting behind bulletproof glass prompts me, through a much-too-low slot, to place my hands on a rectangular, transparent plastic panel: four fingers of the right hand, four fingers of the left hand and then both thumbs. A green light signals that the prints have been registered.

I am then greeted by an employee, a man with a serious expression, a striped shirt and round glasses. Two Chinese women are shooed away from a tiny corner table and we sit down. They now have to stand but are allowed to listen in on our conversation.

11

In silence, he flicks through the copies of my visa application. Without wasting time on small talk, he begins the test.

"The person inviting you, Ms. Wang, is she your friend?"

"Yes, a friend."

"A normal friend or...?" A telling look, man to man.

"Normal friend," I reply.

"You write travel books, about Russia and Iran. You are really famous," he says. The man is well informed, as there is no mention of my being an author in my application.

"Oh, no, not really famous," I answer.

"Do you intend to write a book about China?"

"No," I reply.

If I were to say anything else, he could demand I fill out an application for a journalist's visa. A different office is responsible for this, and they don't have a reputation for being particularly forthcoming. For the entire three-month trip, I would have to state in advance all the proposed topics to be covered and all the planned interview partners.

I can't do that, as I have no idea yet who I am going to meet.

"Do you plan to travel a lot inside the country?"

"Just two cities: Shanghai and Chengdu," I claim.

I want to travel right across the country, from the high-tech metropolis of Shenzhen to the capital Beijing, from the province of Liaoning on the border with North Korea to Yunnan province on the border with Myanmar.

"To Chengdu? With Ms. Wang?"

"No, alone. I want to eat plenty of hot pot there."

"Can you eat spicy food?"

"Yes, but as spicy as in Sichuan? Not every day."

Not even a hint of a smile. The subject of food normally works on all Chinese people; this man is apparently immune.

The two displaced ladies are now at the counter and talking excitedly through the glass panel; something seems to be wrong with their visa papers. Consulates are modern-day drawbridges. Here, fortresses are defended, people classified as "desirable" or "undesirable." In China's case, in particular, a consulate is also a place of maximum individuality, as here, and only here, is it suggested that in a country of 1.4 billion can one person actually make a difference.

Back to the questions.

"You were also in China in 2014—where exactly?"

"Shanghai, Beijing, Xi'an, Xinjiang province, once in a train straight across the country from east to west."

"Where were you in Xinjiang?"

"In the capital, Ürümqi."

"Aha, also in Kashgar?"

"Yes, also in Kashgar."

"Are you planning to make another trip to Xinjiang?"

Xinjiang is the province in the northwest that is in crisis because the government has established "reeducation," or internment, camps for Muslims as well as a surveillance system unequaled in the world. Here, China shows its ugly side.

Of course I want to go to Xinjiang.

"No," I say. "Just Shanghai and Chengdu. Above all, I want to improve my language skills on this trip."

"You will be hearing from the visa authorities."

· · · · · · · · · ·

MY DESIRE TO get to know China better doesn't contradict Xi Jinping Thought on Socialism With Chinese Characteristics for a New Era, the collected wisdom of the head of state. But I still had to go through that charade at the consulate.

The future number one world power is concerned with one single traveler who is not seeking access to secret documents, is not intending to incite revolution, is not planning to murder anybody but just wants to travel a bit through the country and write down his experiences.

If the visa application is successful, then I think it will be a farewell visit, as it is highly unlikely that I will be able to get another one after the book is published. Because I want to know more about this country than they are willing to divulge. The word "understand" can be interpreted so differently.

I log on to the travel portal Couchsurfing.com to look for hosts. Globally, millions of members offer free accommodation, and more than 857,000 members are registered in China.

Yang is astonished at the high number. "Most Chinese don't trust strangers," she says when we meet again. "They trust their friends but not someone they have just met. I fear that this journey will be a traumatic experience for you."

"Last time you said that once I was there, the sky's the limit."

"The one doesn't exclude the other. But to be successful you have to first become *gaofushuai*."

"What?"

"*Gao fu shuai*. Tall, rich and handsome. The Chinese term for a perfect man."

Yang eyes up the mini kitchen in my two-room apartment, then me from top to bottom, and adds: "Well, you're certainly tall."

Okay, maybe the missing attributes can be corrected. For *fu* I decide to start my journey in the casino paradise of Macau. For *shuai* I download two Chinese photo editing apps called Pitu and MyIdol that promise beautifying filters and 3-D avatar creations. Additionally, I reserve a spot in a Chinese language course, get my respirator mask out of the closet, buy fifteen packs of Lübeck marzipan for my hosts and purchase a VPN program for my cell phone that will allow me to access blocked websites throughout the world.

One day in March, I receive the liberating call from the Chinese consulate in the posh Elbchaussee: my passport with visa awaits collection.

To: Yang Berlin
Hooray! It worked! I'm going to China!

From: Yang Berlin
Don't forget to return with both kidneys haha

MILLIONAIRES IN TRACKSUITS

FOUR WEEKS LATER, I land at Macau International Airport, a rather small representative of its kind with only ten gates. Arriving there feels a bit like landing on an aircraft carrier, as, because of lack of space, the runway is on a 2.25-mile-long artificial island in the South China Sea. Compared to the other passengers, I appear tall, fair-haired and blue-eyed. And not particularly *fu*; many people are wearing wristwatches and carrying handbags costing many times the price of my plane ticket.

Everyone flocks to the free shuttle buses with colorful signs advertising Wynn Palace, Venetian or Grand Lisboa. You shouldn't keep luck waiting, so why go to the hotel first when public transport will deliver you directly to the games table? Most casinos are integrated into large hotels with all the necessary frills available, so now staunch gamblers don't even have to venture out into the bleak, smoggy springtime heat of the real world.

I contacted eight potential hosts, seven of whom, according to their profiles, were somehow connected professionally to casinos. I hoped to get some advice from them for my plan to become incredibly rich in a very short time. The eighth was May, and she hates casinos, and only she replied with an invitation to stay. Even host seeking is a game of chance here.

From May's profile I know that she has traveled to twenty-five different countries, she works in the human resources department of an airline and she worships the filmmaker Wong Kar-wai. I liked her philosophy for life: Be like a child but not childish.

I still have a few hours before I'm going to meet up with her, so I take the bus to the Grand Lisboa. Casinos seem to be a good starting point on the long path to understanding China—money and superstition carry much weight here, so the players at the gaming tables must be fully in their element. On mainland China, gambling is forbidden, which is why there is an enormous crush here.

The gambling halls of Macau represent the frantic development of China in the last thirty years. Communist ideals are replaced by the chance for any individual to win a sudden ascent. There are ludicrous prospects of success alongside considerable risks, and the aim to assume a leading role worldwide—revenues from Macau's casinos are almost five times those from Las Vegas. China's special administrative region is roughly the size of Key West but has the third-largest gross domestic product per capita in the world.

Right next to the airport, the bus passes the construction site of a subway line with driverless trains that is due to start service in a couple of months and a brand-new ferry terminal with nineteen jetties and 127 passport control counters. Just at this terminal they are expecting 30 million visitors a year.

17

Another passenger terminal can be found a bit farther north. The urban planners want tourists that are like the mah-jongg tiles at one of the fully automated tables—first there is a slight rumbling and clattering noise, then a hatch opens and there they are, ready all in a row so that the game can begin without delay.

Soon I can make out the illuminated skyline of the Macau peninsula beyond the oil-filmed waters.

The new Grand Lisboa casino stands out clearly amid the other skyscrapers, a building that manages, despite its blossom shape and gold lighting, to look as threatening as a huge god of vengeance made of concrete and glass.

The bus stops. I enter the perfumed entrance hall through some sliding doors and deposit my backpack at reception. One games table next to another stands on the deep pile red carpet, mostly offering baccarat and a Chinese dice game, sic bo. Also there are endless rows of slot machines with names like Mighty Dragon, Golden Goddess and Lucky Empress. Semispherical surveillance cameras hang from golden gantries, customers are reflected in brass-colored ATMs and in the shiny garbage cans, everything glistens and blinks, beckons and promises. There is no dress code, which is why unrestrained people-watching comes directly after trying to get incredibly rich as the second-best way to pass time in the Grand Lisboa.

Without claiming to be empirically exact, I discover that those wearing business suits have the worst manners, that men in athletic gear compensate for being underdressed by placing high bets and that sporting an NBA tank top with a Breitling wristwatch is just as acceptable as using a Hello Kitty handbag as a receptacle for your gaming chips worth as much as a three-room apartment. I watch as a young man, not even twenty-five years old and wearing a hoodie, yawns frequently while placing 15,000 Hong Kong dollar chips (US$1,900) per game—for some reason, HKD are used instead of Macau pataca (MOP). In turns, and with panache, he slams his chip and then the game-deciding card down on the baize.

After three unsuccessful rounds of baccarat in a row, he has no chips in front of him, just a credit card, which he gathers before slowly strolling towards the cashier's window. I stroll, in turn, towards the exit to take a cab to my prearranged meeting place with May.

My destination is the southern end of the Ponte da Amizade, or Friendship Bridge. Streets still bear Portuguese names, though most people speak Cantonese. The city-state was a Portuguese colony for 442 years and has belonged to China again only since 1999.

A young woman in a floral dress with black straps and a stiff white blouse approaches me waving. I will never understand why people who are less than a few feet away from each other need to wave at each other. But here I'm obviously thinking too European; in Asia, handshakes are not so common.

"Hello May, nice to meet you!" I say, and with a slight delay, wave back.

"Same here! I hope you haven't come to gamble," she says.

"What have you got against casinos?" I ask.

"They are ruining the city. Many of the locals don't even bother going to university because jobs in the casinos are much more lucrative. And all these new buildings are not good for wildlife. In winter, rare birds from Siberia come here, but because of the light pollution, there are fewer and fewer every year."

19

We pass a security guard and enter May's housing estate, consisting of twelve almost identical high-rise buildings, an outdoor swimming pool and a tennis court with Astroturf. We reach the entranceway with a polished marble floor framed by two Greek columns; next to the elevator is an oil painting of a female cellist in a gold frame hanging a bit askew.

Her apartment on the eighth floor seems equally opulent, with expensive parquet floor, leather sofas and a huge TV. The housekeeper is hanging up clothes on the balcony. May lives here with her brother, whom I don't get to meet. In one corner is a cabinet full of cups, medals and commendations for special accomplishments at school.

"All yours?" I ask.

"Roughly half of them," she says, but her smile, half-modest, half-proud, suggests that she is minimizing.

"I was a goody-goody."

"A what?"

"A goody-goody, teacher's pet. I always had the best grades."

When speaking, May often rubs her chin or nods devoutly, which looks very erudite. She's twenty-eight and speaks perfect American English; she studied linguistics in Portland, Oregon, for a couple of years.

She leads me through an enormous kitchen to a small room that will be mine for the next two days. There is a bed and a couple of shelves with kettles, irons and cleaning materials.

We take a cab into the old part of the city of Taipa, which is only a few minutes' walk away from the largest casino district. Taipa is one of the original three separate Macau islands, which have since been linked by land reclamation schemes and bridges. Because it lacks tall buildings, Taipa adds nothing to Macau's skyline, but it does have quaint little alleyways with pubs and shops offering almond cookies, herbal teas and cigarettes with obvious typos in their brand names.

We reach a wonderful park with croaking frogs and chirping cicadas. "This is Macau. A mixture of old and new, natural and artificial, beauty and craziness," says May. She points to the flashing gambling hotels. "A couple of decades ago, that was all sea." Where the oyster fishers were once the only ones trying their luck, is now covered by a number of square miles of artificial land for the casinos.

Keeping vigil in the park is a golden statue of the Portuguese poet and adventurer Luís de Camões, who was a chief warrant officer in Macau in the sixteenth century. I ask, half-jokingly, whether he was a gambler.

"He traveled by ship between Europe and Asia—in his time, that was similar to gambling but more like Russian roulette," she replies.

The golden-floodlit Camões is holding his head down as if he can't bear the view of the casinos and one hand up, with fingers spread, in a silent eternal reproach. *What on earth have you done to my city?*

"The famous Portuguese *saudade*, a kind of melancholy and nostalgia, runs through many of his works," says May.

I ask her what she yearns for when she gazes at her city.

"I would love to live in Europe, because there are so many good museums there," she says.

· · · · · · · · · ·

THE NEXT DAY, after May has gone to work, I go to the biggest casino in the world. The Venetian Macau is a bigger copy of the Las Vegas Venetian, which copied the architecture of the Italian city of Venice, and this is saying quite a lot about the global shift in aspirations of economic supremacy.

The complex is built on sand; more than 1 million tons were deposited here. In addition to the actual hotel building, which is boomerang shaped, there is a crimson replica of St. Mark's Campanile. From here, after crossing the Rialto Bridge, you can be at the Eiffel Tower in five minutes by foot. In front of me unfolds a perfect reproduction of the Doge's Palace, and by the main entrance, Vivaldi's *Four Seasons* emanate from loudspeakers attached to a lamppost. Between Gothic pillars (left and right); polished marble (below); and vivid, luminous ceiling paintings featuring heroes, goddesses and horses (above), I work my way to the North restaurant near the casino entrance.

Red lanterns at the windows, red porcelain on the tables and red silk waistcoats on the waitresses all make it patently clear what the lucky color is here. Superstitious Chinese people wear red underwear while gambling and know a couple of other tricks that apparently increase their chances of winning: leaving lights on in the hotel room, never entering a casino through the main entrance and, on the way there, not meeting a monk or a nun. Also, newly opened games palaces promise less success than those that are a few years old.

With so much red in the restaurant there can be little doubt about my impending wealth, and correspondingly, the waitress opens the menu to a list of spirits from the last century. The fifty-year-old Kweichow Moutai, at 53 percent alcohol, costs just over US$9,000. I decide this is a good time to get used to the customary hot water with my meal, which comes without charge. I order a portion of *mapo doufu*, a popular spicy dish from Sichuan province, to go with it.

The guests at the other tables, deep in concentration, are working through illustrated menus, acting more like addicts than people seeking information, rapidly leafing from one page to the next, so that the transition wastes as few hundredths of a second as possible, faces almost touching the laminated sheets as if every detail could be definitive. No single moment should be squandered on non-viewing of the dishes. Those familiar with Chinese cuisine can appreciate this fully. By "Chinese cuisine," I don't mean the sweet-and-sour-pork-MSG-laden-fortune-cookie dives where every order of B1 or M4 is an insult to the cultural heritage of the homeland, mostly under the auspices of an outwardly-stoically-doing-what-it-is-supposed-to-be-doing-but-inwardly-depressed beckoning cat. Next time you see one, look a little more closely at its face; you don't need a degree in psychology to sense the sadness.

But back to the place where they make Chinese food properly. *Mapo doufu* consists of minced pork, tofu and Sichuan pepper that, when seasoned skillfully, creates a quasi-erotic mélange for diners. With each bite, the lips tingle a bit more, almost to the point of numbness. Ideally, like today, the spiciness is calibrated such that the consumer occasionally has to

23

raise his nose but is not reduced to tears. The tingling sensation returns now and then after the meal, but gradually, the waves become weaker. I wonder how often I would have to eat *mapo doufu* to always have the tingling effect, but it would make for a life that was pretty low on vitamins.

I pay and head to the games tables. I studied the rules for *sic bo* on the internet; they are quite simple: Three dice and the player bets on the total. You can also try to predict the exact total, three twos or three threes or individual dice calls. The possible returns vary according to the probability. Most of the betting, however, is on *xiao* or *da*, small or big, totals of up to and including ten and numbers from eleven upwards. The payout, if you win, is double the stake.

For 1,000 MOP I can get 1,000 HKD (US$127) in chips. I then go to a table where there are already a number of people and place 300 HKD on *da*, big.

The dice clatter, the croupier lifts the golden shaker: five, five and six—altogether sixteen. I won! If I were clever, I would stop then, but of course I carry on. Next round I place three hundred on *xiao*, small, and then three hundred on odd number and lose both times.

Frustrated, I take a short break, but in my mind I continue playing. The mean thing about games of chance is the simplicity, the mind games. The gambler mentality doesn't come about when playing but during the times between. I begin to imagine recognizing patterns in the results, having the situation under control. In this fantasy, I place massive bets and interpret every result as confirmation of my expertise: *Look, I would have won a fortune there*, or *Ha, really clever to have skipped that round*. That, by the way, is a very Western view of the games table. According to surveys, we are more likely to believe that destiny lies in our own hands than the Chinese, who view destiny as an external force that can only be influenced indirectly with the aid of good luck charms.

On we go. Three hundred on *xiao*: won; three hundred on *da*: won again. Have I managed to see through *sic bo*? Will this run of luck last forever? I will never know, because I quit and get my 1,300 HKD. My winnings? Roughly US$38. Just enough for a ticket to the mainland.

Megacities That (Almost) Nobody Knows

	City	Population
1	Zhengzhou, Henan province	10.1 million
2	Jinan, Shandong province	8.7 million
3	Shenyang, Liaoning province	8.3 million
4	Dongguan, Guangdong province	8.2 million
5	Changchun, Jilin province	7.7 million
6	Tangshan, Hebei province	7.5 million
7	Shantou, Guangdong province	5.4 million
8	Guiyang, Guizhou province	4.7 million
9	Changzhou, Jiangsu province	4.6 million
10	Taiyuan, Shanxi province	4.2 million

Then I take a look at Venice, which is just one escalator up and consists of long aisles with Gothic facades housing high-fashion and handbag shops. Even the Grand Canal has been reproduced, the bright blue waters traversed by gondoliers who churn out opera arias surprisingly adeptly. They sing "'O *sole mio*" with no sun in sight, but instead an illuminated ceiling simulates radiantly blue sky with cotton-ball clouds. This is surely popular. There was once a survey of Chinese travel bloggers on what they liked about Europe and "blue sky" was very high on the list, as it is a rare phenomenon here.

Tourist groups from Shanghai and Chengdu are gathered at the St. Mark's Square repro, wearing red caps and taking photos just like the many Chinese tourists at the real thing. Behind the facades they can shop at Victoria's Secret, Swarovski or Koi Kei Bakery. All the sales staff speak their language, the selfie backgrounds are sensational and Chinese food tastes better here than in Europe, which begs the question, why go to the real Italy?

Later, May tells me about her brother and sisters who really wouldn't find a convincing argument for going there. "They are not interested in the world outside, just in shopping and consumption. Although they had the chance, they chose not to study abroad. I don't understand them, and they don't understand me," she explains.

She has four sisters and one brother and is the second youngest. Her parents were not particularly fond of China's one-child policy. "When I was a baby there were no computers and my mother was clever. She always claimed at the administrative offices that we had moved a few times and that the receipts for the paid fines for the extra children had been mislaid. We never had to pay."

We drive to the southern neighborhood of Coloane in her angular Toyota minivan. Past bamboo scaffolding and green latticed awnings behind which a new, grand building is emerging. Past already existing grand buildings, symbols of a wealth that seemed unthinkable here a few decades ago.

May talks of her father. Although this modest, reflective young lady doesn't seem to fit in with the new Macau, her family's story is typical of the rapid growth of the region. "My father came from a village in the Guangdong province where he only went to elementary school. His family was poor, as everyone was then. First of all, he worked for a butcher, then as a delivery boy taking goods on his motorbike to the nearest city: Zhaoqing."

We drive past a row of huge letters at the side of the road, which spell out: "City of Dreams."

"My dad noticed that there were very few motorbikes with loading space to transport things from the village to the city," May continues. "So he took out credit, bought a couple of bikes and employed a couple of riders."

Outside, the sunlight is reflected in the blue glass of the Studio City casino complex. At the center of the eight-building compound are the rotating passenger pods of a Ferris wheel in the form of the Chinese lucky number eight. So, just like the punters behind the glass placing their bets on *da* or *xiao*, May's father took out credit for motorbikes as a bet on the future, but having the right instinct was the deciding factor, not just relying on pure luck.

"For the first time in his life, my father had a decent income. He also noticed how society was changing and new demands were emerging. People wanted to have their own motorbikes. In the mid-eighties, he opened up a shop named *xingfu motuoche*—motorbikes of joy—which sold motorbikes with space for transporting goods. If you mention the name in my village today, everybody knows it." 27

As if to underline her words, on our right, next to a golf course, a couple of go-karts having a race buzz past.

"He earned enough money to move to the city. There he started dealing in real estate. He bought land, built high-rises and sold apartments."

"Casinos, too?"

"No, he would never do that. My parents think gambling is dishonest. They are sad that my brother has recently gotten a job in a casino, even though he only works in the bonus points department."

May parks the car near the sea promenade. Coloane, once the most southerly island of the city-state but now linked to the rest, couldn't feel more different from the world of high-rise buildings only a five-minute drive away. It has the feel of a fishing village, with colonial buildings, small alleyways, a Christian chapel and a number of Taoist temples. A couple of streets are untarred dirt tracks, and on the shore sit the abandoned ruins of the huge Lai Chi Vun shipyard. Up to well into the 1990s, thousands of craftsmen built wooden fishing junks here, but then the competition from the mainland, with their metal boats and automated manufacturing processes, became too stiff. Only the steel skeleton remains of the Coloane dockyard halls. They act as outdated memorials to a brutal competitive rivalry in which aesthetics and honest craftsmanship came second. Massive planks and bits of corrugated iron are lying around, and it stinks of damp wood and solvents.

We sit in a café that once provided the workers with cookies and warm drinks and now sells tourists coffee with condensed milk. A picture of Mao Zedong hangs on the wall, with the wish that he will live to be ten thousand years old. In his day, shipbuilding here was still flourishing.

"Probably the ruins of the wharf will be demolished soon," says May resignedly. "They want to build an amusement park so that even more tourists will come here."

28

From: Simone Shenzhen

Hi Stephan, we would be happy to invite you to Shenzhen :)
We have 5 cats and you would have to share a small living
room with them. Is that ok for you?
Greetings, Simone and Diego

To: Simone Shenzhen

I like cats, sounds interesting! Thanks for the invitation and
see you soon!

THE ELECTRIC CITY

MAY DRIVES ME back to the ferry terminal, where we say our good-byes. I buy a ticket with my casino winnings and board a blue-and-white hydrofoil called *Xunlong 3* bound for Shenzhen. As everyone talks of "mainland China," I rather liked the idea of reaching this mysterious entity by boat. On top of this, I knew as a kid that China should always be approached by sea routes, because that's the way they do it in the popular German children's novel *Jim Button and Luke the Engine Driver*.

The seats are blotched, it smells like vomit and noodle soup, and mud-colored waves raise and lower the boat in four-four time. Plastic red letters dangle from the ceiling wishing everyone a "Happy Spring Festival." To begin, we speed alongside the Hong Kong–Zhuhai–Macau Bridge, a road link over artificial islands and a tunnel totaling some thirty-five miles. As if there weren't enough ways of reaching Macau, they built the longest fixed link in the world right here.

There is an ad from the producers of face masks being shown on a TV screen, and in my head the poetic English subtitles blend with beat of the ship's hull: "International Assembly. Aseptic Packaging. Founder Chen. Customer Feedback. You Deserve It."

Ah, yes, the face. My *gaofushuai* mission. In Macau, the *fu* part didn't really work out, so let's see what I can do for the visuals—the *shuai*. My cell phone signals a notification—"low security" on Wi-Fi, but the transmission quality is perfect. Breaking news informs me that the Chinese National People's Congress has voted to lift the presidential two-term limit for Xi Jinping. Now, he can remain in power until he dies. Well, haven't I chosen an interesting day for my arrival?

I open the Pitu app, which greets me with the message: "Please put your face in the frame." A rectangular frame appears on the screen, and by the third attempt, I manage to make a reasonably realistic self-portrait. Now I have hundreds of ways of morphing my face onto those of movie stars, comic figures or legendary heroes. There are categories like "Demigods and Demons," "Christmas Dreams" and "Springtime Beauty." Such childish nonsense, I'm really *much* too old for all this. But just for the sake of trying, I transform my digital alter ego into an ancient Chinese swordsman, an elf with spiky ears, Bran from *Game of Thrones*, a chubby baby and a rapper in a Bruce Lee T-shirt (in my mind, I keep hearing the words: *Customer feedback. You deserve it.*).

On the screen my skin is very pink, the eyes slightly larger than life and the eyebrows perfectly plucked. Everything is automatically optimized, and I look ten years younger. As this kind of brutal beautification is highly trendy in China, it has its own term: *wanghonglian*, which roughly translated means: "internet celebrity face." You wouldn't be able to recognize many stars in real life because their online identities appear

31

doe-eyed and soft-focused. With my skincare cream model's face, and in the traditional clothing of the Zhuang ethnic group, I already feel very Chinese and save my new profile picture in the messenger program WeChat.

When I look up from my cell phone forty-five minutes later, we are just off Shenzhen. To the right, silos and red-and-white-striped chimneys; to the left, derricks and shipping containers. The skyline of the megacity that is home to 12 million looks glassy and cold in the mist, but soon a huge terminal painted in five colors takes up the field of vision. We dock near the equally large *Costa Atlantica*, one of many European ships that are used exclusively in China. Worldwide there is no cruise ship market that is growing faster, with the number of passengers carried already second place behind the USA.

I pass through the Temperature Monitoring facility, which automatically measures the body temperature of arrivals, and am then led to the fingerprint machine. "Welcome to China" appears on the screen. Left hand. Right hand. Both thumbs. I wonder whether someone cleans the glass before the next arrival slaps their fingers on it.

At passport counter number five, the one for "foreigners," the official wants another print of my thumb to compare it with the automated image. He scans my passport but doesn't look at my face, because matching is done by a high-resolution camera. After I get two stamps and my passport back, a console with a touch screen prompts me to assess the official: "Perfect," "Good," "Took too long," or "Bad service." I choose "Perfect," and I'm through.

A silent shuttle bus takes me to the Shekou Port subway station. In Shenzhen, all 16,359 public buses have been battery powered since January 2018. An equally silent escalator takes me to the subway security gates. The train cars, as clean as a hospital floor, are covered in ads for the newest electric SUVs from a company called GAC Motors.

I get out after two stops. Up on the main street I see a number of angular blue e-cabs from BYD, a company from Shenzhen that began by making batteries and later the cars for them to go into. Roughly 12,500 municipal cabs already use rechargeable batteries, which is one hundred times as many as in all of Germany at the moment.

There is no place that symbolizes China's boom better than Shenzhen. The once sleepy fishing village on the south Chinese coast received its town charter only in 1980, and the government created a special economic zone there to compete with Hong Kong in the distant future. Quite an ambitious idea—the still British colony had 5 million inhabitants then; Shenzhen, with thirty thousand, was hardly more than a village.

"Let in the West Wind. Wealth is glorious,"[1] was the motto of Deng Xiaoping, who was the leader of the Communist Party after Mao Zedong's death and the end of the Cultural Revolution.

Under his leadership, between 1978 and 1992, China began a new era geared towards capitalism. In Shenzhen, firms and jobs were created, and the value of property multiplied; the locals could sell their land for state construction projects for incredible sums. Shenzhen has become the only place in China where an affirmative answer to the question "Are you from the village?" is guaranteed to gain great respect from the person making the inquiry because they are probably talking to a millionaire. The city authorities built highways and tower blocks, wanting to be modern at all costs. Sometimes they went a bit too far—for example, wanting to ban bikes completely for being old-fashioned.

This development, at least, has been revoked. On every corner now there are hire bikes; in one side street they are even piled on top of one another—about a hundred yellow and silvery-orange specimens. The market leaders, Ofo and Mobike, operate without docking stations, just with GPS, and clients can abandon them wherever they wish within the city limits. This is practical, but it has its disadvantages, as during the night, transporters gather the bikes up for the sake of tidiness, but the companies are still having trouble keeping up with demand. Although good for the environment, they often detract from the look of a neighborhood—the dilemma of wind turbines and solar panels now also applies to hire bikes.

At the prearranged street corner, Simone and Diego approach: two cheery-looking figures around thirty, wearing shorts and sneakers. Simone's given name is Zidan, but like

34

many people of her generation, she chose a second Western name when she started learning English. The results often sound as though the English-language novices experimented with LSD for inspiration, choosing names like Sugar, Honey, Candy, Bunny, Happy, Flower or Monday. Diego, however, was given his name at birth; he's from Colombia and lived in England for quite a while. In Shenzhen, he works as an advertising video producer, and Simone is an art teacher.

The usual getting-to-know-you small talk is dropped, as I meet the couple in the middle of a lively discussion about Snow White. Simone thinks that the fairy tale is totally unsuitable for children. "The prince kisses a dead minor, so it's about both pedophilia and necrophilia. What's wrong with you Europeans?" She shoots a critical look in my direction.

I can't think of a convincing argument, so I try a few whataboutisms: "Come on, you Chinese change the words of 'Frère Jacques' to make a song poking fun at disabled animals. What are kids supposed to learn from that?" The Chinese text I learned in a language course goes like this: "Two big tigers, two big tigers, run very fast, run very fast, one of them has no eyes, one of them has no tail, what a laugh, what a laugh."

"Probably there is some hidden truth about both our countries lurking in there somewhere," says Simone, who studied in Switzerland for a couple of years.

There is no doubt about her love for animals. A rattling escalator brings us to their apartment on the eleventh floor of a weather-beaten high-rise where I get to know Mitzi, Munchi, Alba, Pickwick and Pumpkin, the four-legged roommates with whom I will be sharing the living room. Every possible place to sit is so thick with cat fur that my merino sweater now knows how it feels to be a schnitzel coated in breadcrumbs. But I was warned, and I'm well aware that I haven't booked into a five-star hotel. The sofa and bookshelves have been made catproof with blankets. There is an opulent mouse-gray scratching post in one corner and three closed designer litter boxes look like three parallel robot heads made of white plastic. Three adults and five animals in 430 square feet—it sure is going to be cozy.

But first, we ride the subway downtown for a couple of craft beers at the Glass Hammer Brewing Co. In the style of a British pub, with meager lighting, it has a thirty-foot-long bar and offers forty-six beers from the barrel, most produced in the house brewery. We find a table on the veranda with a view of the metallic facade of the 115-story Ping An skyscraper, which after Shanghai Tower, is the second-tallest building in China and the fourth tallest in the world. The bar next door has aquariums housing real sharks integrated into its facade. We order beers called Forgotten Dreams and Wonderwall, and Simone asks the waiter whether there is a power bank to charge her cell phone. "I think I have enough points not to have to leave a deposit," she says. The waiter scans her phone and she does have enough—more than 700 from a possible 950 points with Sesame Credit. And with that, she is considered trustworthy enough.

Sesame Credit is a credit scoring app from the Alibaba Group, the biggest IT company in China. Participation is voluntary, but those who behave themselves can relatively easily get small amounts of credit from banks and don't have to leave a deposit when hiring bikes, borrowing power banks or even renting umbrellas. A high number of points has advantages on some dating apps and can even help to jump the line when visiting the doctor. It is similar to collecting payback bonus points, but the real collector is Alibaba. Sesame

Credit, the twenty-first-century equivalent of the command "Open sesame," allows Ali Baba to open the door to treasures more valuable than gold and diamonds together—the data of Chinese consumers. And that information is not only stored on the servers of the business; the state authorities also have access to it.

The waiter scans Simone's phone again and the beers are paid for. Diego remembers that he owes her a couple of yuan. He sends it to her in a digital red envelope via a WeChat message that takes a few seconds. When I pay for the next round, I have to fish around awkwardly in my wallet for a couple of crumpled banknotes. I feel behind the times, as if I had just presented my hosts with a cassette mixtape and then asked them for directions to the nearest telephone booth. A long time ago, the Chinese invented paper money; now they are on the verge of being the first to abandon it.

"I never take cash when I go out," says Simone. "People are lazy, so naturally I do what is easiest." But the company's data hoarding worries her. "Sometimes I baidu something, and then later when I'm on the Taobao site, the very thing I was looking for is offered to me. They've got some nerve simply passing on my customer information," she complains. Baidu is the equivalent of Google, which is blocked in China, and Taobao is like a mixture of eBay and Amazon.

The development of Sesame Credit, and other such apps, will soon enable an almost complete surveillance of the population. "The gentleman understands what is moral, the small man what is profitable," was known to Confucius.[2] *Let's merge the two*, thought the Communist Party, and came up with the social credit system that is soon to be introduced nationwide.

Here you can lose points by failing to pay your debts on time, for example, or driving through red traffic lights or visiting online porn sites. Conversely, those who pay rent punctually, save a child or report a crime are rewarded with points. It is almost as if somebody is sitting somewhere judging every living moment, then rating it with: good, medium or bad. Life becomes a computer game, with video referee and constant appraisal. Some people might enjoy it, but failure has direct consequences: those who score badly are less likely to obtain credit, are forced to pay more for insurance or, in extreme cases, are not allowed to travel by train or plane. The ultimate tool to control people's behavior and to reduce criminality but also to demand unconditional obedience to the state.

A number of cities are already running pilot schemes where even political opinions are incorporated into the ratings. "It's all about what you have posted online and how your friends respond," says Simone. "If you are married, then you are considered relatively 'stable.' With children, more so. But if a friend of mine criticizes the government on Weibo, it will also affect my points in the future. It's crazy that such plans haven't caused an international outcry, isn't it? Cheers."

On the way home, my hosts show me a red-light district that is only two streets away from where they live. Shenzhen was long known as "second wife city," because rich men from Hong Kong played sugar daddy and financed their concubines' apartments and visits to the shopping mall. As the cost of living in Shenzhen creeps ever closer to that of the neighboring city, however, the practice has declined. But prostitution, though officially forbidden, seems to be flourishing. We pass bars with names like Titty Twister, China Dolls and the Why Not Bar but resist the luring calls of the heavily made-up doorway sirens and the purred offers of "massagies" from casual side-street would-be acquaintances.

Diego wants to show me his favorite place on the street. Through an inconspicuous door we enter a room in which a number of men are standing in front of a sheet of glass, inspecting an international range of beauties while being watched by surveillance cameras. Blonde or brown, light or dark, the prices are directly below the goods, and payment is made via WeChat. "It even works without proof of age," says Diego. Paulaner, Erdinger, Leffe, Guinness and many other brands are at the ready behind the window. "In China you can get almost anything from machines, even beer. Crazy, isn't it?" He then taps in a code for three cans of Kronenbourg 1664, for the way home. Diego's favorite attraction in the red-light district is a machine.

In my life I've been caught in the flash of speed cameras a few times and know precisely the four phases my mind shoots through in the ensuing milliseconds: surprise → anger at the overzealous cops → worried glance at the speedometer → resignation. This sequence is so inculcated that being flashed by a camera on the sidewalk causes considerable irritation. It happens between the red-light street and a less shady neighboring road. Walking too quickly? Routine face check? Suspicion of visiting a brothel? I can find no plausible explanation but suspect it is one of the last two options. Just to check that the alcohol hasn't clouded my judgment, I walk back. Another flash. And, because now it really doesn't matter anymore, and because that last beer was one too many, I walk by one more time, with a big smile. At least they'll have something to laugh at. The high-resolution box-shaped camera, made by Hikvision, comes from the city of Hangzhou and is the worldwide leader in surveillance technology. The company doesn't have to worry about sales volume in the coming years. Several hundred million such cameras are in operation in China, and there is still demand for more.

Motorists, by the way, are recorded constantly on all the major streets, not only to catch them driving too fast but also to see whether they are wearing seat belts and just to keep an eye on where they are cruising around. As I learn later, sometimes there are flashes without photos being taken, simply to send the message: *Hey, we're watching what you're up to.*

I will never find out whether and where my three pedestrian films are stored. But I can spot surveillance cameras that are on 24-7 on every street corner. There will be a film version of this trip recorded somewhere, without my having to take a cameraperson, with hours and hours of material of streets, railway stations and parks. Somebody just has to make the effort to edit it.

At home Diego sets up a camp cot for me in the middle of the living room. Soon I'm alone with five energetic cats who don't seem to realize the connection between lights out and sleep. They climb up the curtains, jump over the sofa and camp cot, racing back and forth from the scratching post to my backpack, mewing and spitting, wrangling and fighting. I lie there like a living prop at a *Gulliver's Travels*–themed costume party and mull over what a load of perfect-world nonsense the cartoon *Simon's Cat* is. One single bloody cat—boy, oh boy, that guy had problems.

Pickwick decides to use my elbow as a starting ramp for a reckless jump. The claws of the cat's hind legs catch the skin, and I'm left with two red scratches and blood dripping onto my T-shirt. I grab my phone. The internet diagnoses toxoplasmosis, cat-scratch disease, tetanus or, at the very least, blood poisoning. Somewhere deep inside my backpack I find some antiseptic spray. The party around me goes on for hours.

"How was it with the cats?" asks Simone in the morning as she shuffles out of the bedroom and sees Pickwick, Alba and Pumpkin innocently dozing at my feet.

"Interesting," I reply truthfully, while hiding my abused elbow under the sheets.

· · · · · · · · · ·

DURING THE DAY, Simone and Diego both have something to do, so I explore the city on my own. On the Couchsurfing site I created a "public trip" so that other members could see that I am in Shenzhen and would enjoy meeting some locals. One person responded and left her WeChat contact details: Qing, thirty-four, a policewoman. Her job makes me a bit suspicious. Particularly here, as I have never seen a place with so many security cameras. So, as a foreign journalist, am I about to be allocated a minder after all? My gut feeling says I should be cautious and cancel the meeting. Especially as she looks pretty. I open up the WeChat message window.

To: Qing Policewoman
Ni hao Qing, I am Stephan from couchsurfing. I would love to meet you! Is 5pm ok?

HIGH TECH
AND HOT POT

DESPITE ITS SPECTACULAR skyscrapers, Shenzhen is not a place of beauty, but at least it has a pretty promenade with a view of Hong Kong and the air quality is better than in most other Chinese megacities. If tourists were less interested in beaches and relaxation and more in a look at the future, then Shenzhen would be their city. They could, for instance, visit the Huaqingbei market, a gigantic electronic toy bazaar, with household robots, telescopic lenses for cell phones, shimmering gold karaoke mics with integrated echo effect and, of course, drones, buzzing around like giant insects, most made by DJI, the industry's world leader from Shenzhen. Also based here is the technology giant Tencent, which transformed WeChat from a simple WhatsApp copy to a universal app for all aspects of life. Nowadays, you can use it to pay for things, organize a wedding, book flights, buy cars and take out insurance, usually at a more reasonable price than its competitors.

Also, the telecommunication giants Huawei and ZTE come from Shenzhen. There are more patent applications from this city than from France and Great Britain together. China is, at the moment, going through a transformation into a country of innovation, especially in the field of digital technology. With the construction of a network of transmission masts with ultrafast 5G technology, China has just managed to overtake the US. By 2030, President Xi Jinping wants China to be number one in the world in the artificial intelligence (AI) sector.

I witness where all this high-tech development can lead at the intersection of Xinzhou Road and Lianhua Road, northwest of the idyllic Lianhuashan Park.

Five Chinese Companies to Know

Alibaba Group. The largest IT company in China to which belong the online shopping platforms Taobao and Tmall, as well as the payment system Alipay, among others.

Tencent. The developer of WeChat, the biggest all-round app, with more than 1 billion users. Additionally, the world's leading video game producer.

Baidu. China's largest search engine, with 65 percent market share. The contents displayed are filtered after consultation with the government.

JD.com. China's answer to Amazon but with an integrated logistical system allowing extremely quick delivery of products nationwide. Many goods are already being delivered by drones.

Didi. A ride-sharing company along the lines of Uber but with more customers—more than 25 million trips are booked daily.

Behind two pedestrian crossing lights, LED screens have been fixed, framed by text in blue: "Shenzhen Traffic Police— we can recognize your face. Intelligent cameras will take your picture if you cross on red." An animation shows a computer comparing heads and an eager policeman at the station viewing umpteen screen pages of personal information. "We have your data" is the subtitle. "We know how often you have broken the law." Then there are a few sample photos of offenders.

45

The appearance of technological perfection is somewhat marred by the notification in the upper right corner of the screen recommending an update to the newest version of Google Chrome. Nevertheless, there is no doubting the efficiency of the technology, as according to the police's own information, almost fourteen thousand jaywalkers have been caught in ten months.

Public display of the red-light offenders is just the first step. In the future, those caught will immediately receive a message on their cell phone that includes an automatic debit for the fine and deducts points in the social credit system.

In the afternoon, I have a meeting with Policewoman Qing. I take an e-cab to the InTown shopping mall in Futian district, where she awaits me.

"There is a hot pot restaurant here that is famous for good service," she says on greeting me. She is wearing a light blue jacket, white jeans and white sneakers, with her hair tied in a ponytail. Analysis by a face recognition software would reveal: oval, almost perfectly symmetrical face, high forehead, slight wrinkling around black eyes, narrow eyebrows, wide nose and small ears.

"How are your hosts?" she asks.

"Great. But their five cats are a bit troublesome—they had a wild party all night long."

We ride the escalator to Haidilao on the fourth floor. The waiting area is equipped with snacks of peanuts and cherry tomatoes, board games and a free manicure service in a creative approach to calming the usual flurry here.

A beaming receptionist greets us, a beaming staff member leads us to our table and her beaming colleague inquires about our well-being. He guides Qing into her chair and ceremoniously presents the menu—a tablet computer in an orange case. China's customer service companies often have two to three times the number of personnel compared to Europe's, but they are seldom as overly friendly as here.

"We're lucky that we are here so early. Sometimes you have to wait more than an hour," says Qing.

Her dainty appearance doesn't really match her voice, which has a sharpness that makes even routine sentences sound like reprimands. Qing speaks perfect English, with a British accent. She studied languages before joining the police, where she met her husband, with whom she has a seven-year-old daughter.

"I now work in a prison," she says. "Sadly, most of my colleagues are not well educated. I am different from them, but I don't show it, or they would think me strange."

A waitress brings us aprons to shield us against the spitting fat and towels to wash our hands. Using the touch screen, Qing orders two kinds of soup—a mild one with mushrooms and a spicy one with tomatoes—which are placed on stoves in the middle of the table. On top of these she orders the raw main course, which we have to cook: slices of lamb fillet, little fish balls, lotus roots, bamboo sprouts, octopus, quail's eggs, napa cabbage—all fresh and high quality. A note from the health authorities on the wall awards the kitchen a straight A for hygiene. Customer ratings on the Dazhong Dianping ("many people evaluation") app give the restaurant 4.7 out of 5 stars.

At the pick-and-mix buffet we can make our own dips from a selection of thirty sauces and spices. People who are worried about not being full can stock up on slices of melon, dragon fruit and cucumber until they burst.

A hint about etiquette—don't point at people with chopsticks, and don't leave chopsticks sticking upright in rice; they look like

47

grave decorations. Every book about China has to have at least one tip on etiquette, so now we've got that behind us.

I tell Qing about the pedestrian crosswalk with the screens. "They like testing new technologies in Shenzhen first because the city is very modern," explains Qing. "The cameras are great—every crime can be solved. At my job, if someone escapes, we know that he won't get far. Wait, I'll show you something."

She gets the newest generation of Huawei cell phone out of her handbag. "Look at the camera." She presses the shutter. "This is a police app that recognizes faces, but you are not in the system yet, for sure."

My paranoia returns in seconds, and in seconds the results are in. My head is a 78 percent match to a black-haired guy from Xinjiang province, and there is a 57 percent chance I am an American called Marc.

"We use this app when we are detaining someone who doesn't want to show his ID card," Qing says. "Recently, just for fun, I scanned a picture of my favorite junior high teacher from a newspaper article, and I actually found him. It was great to meet him again after twenty years."

I try imagining a database with 1.4 billion Chinese faces. Theoretically, you could get the software to categorize the heads according to similarity, and then play them back in time lapse, rather like a flip-book. It would be a work of art: first, there is the illusion that all Chinese people look alike, and then, after a few hundred faces, the opposite becomes apparent as the images change continually and the differences begin to stand out.

Qing shows me another job-specific little helper on her work cell phone. With an app—or rather, A-P-P (the Chinese always pronounce the individual letters)—she can scan license plates. If someone is parked illegally, she can immediately find out who owns the car. Another program with a photo function is designed to report illegal advertising—for instance, street traders dealing in *piao, piao*, or forged invoices with made-up figures for falsifying tax statements. Then there are other little gimmicks, such as an internal point ranking among colleagues.

"Here I can check in with my current location. You can do this every half hour, and you get five points for doing so." She slams her phone down on the table. "Can you believe it? We are the police! And they expect us to be tapping into our phones the whole time." She shows me the current rankings of her colleagues. The front-runner has more than 3,500 points. Qing's score is 1,954 and she is ranked eighth. She tells me it's good to sit in the middle of the pack as she taps in her current location: 1,959 points.

A beaming man or a beaming woman with hands interlocked behind their backs is constantly asking us whether we need anything. At the neighboring table, the waiter is tossing a mass of noodles through the air using both hands, rather like a diabolo juggler, and one of his colleagues is cleaning the recently vacated table with what seem to be kung fu–inspired arm movements.

It is thanks to such performances that the Haidilao restaurant chain is a Chinese success story. Zhang Yong, a twenty-four-year-old factory worker from a village in Sichuan, opened his first restaurant with four tables in 1994. He knew that although the guests were used to good food, they were not used to friendly service. The people who felt that he treated them as friends came again. Zhang had found his niche, and had luck with his timing, as in the nineties, if you had a

49

good business idea, anything was possible. Now Haidilao has more than four hundred branches throughout the country.

At the end of our feast I get an evaluation from Qing: "You've got a very normal character: not too cool, not too loud, and you look very normal," she decides.

"Is that good or bad?" I ask.

"It's good. Mouth, nose, ears—none of them too big or small. Have you had surgery?"

"No!"

"Just asking. In my prison, there are quite a few prostitutes who have had a lot of work done. Breasts, backsides, even hidden places."

"Just between you and me, I don't work as a prostitute."

"Well, actually, it might be a good idea. We could travel around and I'd sell you. Can I be your pimp?"

"Errr…"

"You could easily earn a thousand to two thousand yuan [US$150–300] a night. If your customer is pretty, I get 80 percent; if she's ugly, I get 20 percent."

"I need time to think about it."

"We could be rich," says Qing, and laughs.

In China, you can be whatever you want. I hear Yang's voice in my head and give her five out of five points for foresight.

· · · · · · · · · ·

THE SECOND NIGHT with the cats is more relaxed. After only half an hour of gymnastics, peace reigns. I sleep like a log until 6:30-ish, when Pickwick leaps onto my belly. *Time for breakfast*, says his look, but even if I were in a cooperative mood, I have no idea where his food is stored. He seems to understand this and allows me to doze on.

Eventually, Diego rescues the cats from starvation, and Simone books me a bus ticket to Guangzhou from WeChat because it's cheaper than buying one from the driver. She tells me about her student days in Switzerland, where she read many articles about China that weren't accessible in her own country and began seeing things from a different perspective. But since she's been back, she feels that something was missing from the foreign press coverage of China.

"Most journalists just write what their readers want to read. They leave out a lot, and above all, they write about what is bad. In the West, I met many people who think life in China is just like in North Korea. Utter nonsense."

From: Qing Policewoman
It was nice meeting you. Let me know where you are every now and then

To: Qing Policewoman
Will do. You can come along for a bit of the way

From: Qing Policewoman
Hahaha

From: Qing Policewoman
China is too big and I have a lot to do

SELLING FOR PROS

THE COMPANY NAME on the bus seems humble—"Second Bus Company of Guangdong"—but the white imitation leather seats fitted with four USB sockets per row feel relatively posh. Out the window, I can see high-rise facades in every imaginable variation: Frosted glass reflecting the gray skies. Concrete beige with tall rectangular windows—the bathroom-tile look. Some with lattice walls a whole floor wide that conceal balconies. Others with pillars at the entrance. Ones with staggered floors that look like a bunch of huge shoe boxes. And of course, time and again, reinforced concrete skeletons surrounded by cranes and construction machinery, twenty-story giants in clusters of ten or twelve. Somewhere, there is still space for more high-rise settlements, though the vacancy rates are already huge.

The onboard TV is showing the war movie *Wolf Warrior*, which is about a Chinese soldier named Leng Feng who fights some bad guys as part of the elite unit Wolf Fighters. Buildings and tanks explode, with mercenaries firing all over the place, soldiers running, the Chinese army showing off state-of-the-art military equipment, and the big boss bad guy is Bart, an American with a beard. Leng, and it's no coincidence that his name sounds very similar to Lei Feng, a famous model soldier from the Mao era, finally has a showdown with the bad guy in a steppe-like terrain, fighting it out with knives.

"You want to die for your country, you idiot? Do you know what I fight for? For money!" spouts the American, looking really mean. A short time later, he has Leng in a stranglehold with a knife to his throat.

The struggle seems to be over, but the bad guy makes a decisive mistake, ripping off Leng's red shoulder patch with "I Fight for China" written on it. Leng explodes in patriotic fervor and, with the strength of a wolf, manages with superhuman effort to turn the tables and stick the knife into his opponent's neck before jauntily slapping his patch back onto his shoulder. He returns home a hero and as a reward has a date with the prettiest female soldier.

The sequel, *Wolf Warrior 2*, also vibrates with brutal patriotism. It quickly became the most successful Chinese movie of all time, ahead of another military epic, *Operation Red Sea*. The message is clear: China is once more a world military power, and the public loves to be assured of that, since for many decades most war movies dealt with ignominious defeats, from the Opium Wars to the invasion by Japan.

Nowadays, even the box office charts are an indicator of patriotic passion; of the fifteen highest-grossing films only four are Hollywood blockbusters (*Avengers: Endgame*, *The Fate of the Furious*, *Furious 7* and *Avengers: Infinity War*). The remaining eleven are all Chinese productions from 2015 to 2019, mostly action and comedy flicks because the censorship board doesn't allow anything controversial.

The high-rise facades outside are becoming glassier, more expensive and higher: the bus has reached Guangzhou. *Guang* means broad or extensive; *zhou* means administrative district. The suffix is used pretty extensively; on a map of China, you can find, among others: Fuzhou, Suzhou, Binzhou, Dazhou, Hangzhou, Hezhou, Huizhou, Taizhou, Meizhou, Lanzhou, Liuzhou, Shuozhou, Xuzhou, Quanzhou, Qinzhou, Jingzhou, Xinzhou, Wenzhou, Yangzhou, Ganzhou, Cangzhou, Changzhou, Zhangzhou and Zhengzhou.

I plan to meet my host at the main train station in Guangzhou. Yangwei is a twenty-three-year-old computer expert whose Couchsurfing profile is a genuine work of art. Over fifteen to twenty lines, he has fashioned an image of a cheerful human figure out of precisely placed flags, smileys and other emojis. He writes of himself: "I have black hair, yellow skin and small eyes. 1.386 billion people live in this country. Yes, I'm one of them."

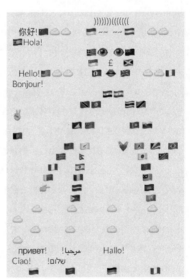

An uninteresting everyman? A boring person like all the others? For me, his strange choice of words and layout extravaganza made him just the opposite. In no other country have I come across so many profiles where people describe themselves as "just a simple guy" or "a normal girl." It might be proof of Confucian modesty and the ideal of fitting in with the majority, of not standing out, not being too individual. Chinese children still learn in school that "a good nail doesn't stick out." But if you instruct people to become standardized, does it mean that various talents and interests are being switched off? I don't think so. And people who describe themselves as "always happy" and "I smile a lot" just tempt me to start looking for the skeletons. Behind low-key facades you can sometimes find great surprises.

We meet at Exit D. Yangwei has all the trappings of the IT guild: black horn-rimmed glasses and an asymmetrical blow-dried hairstyle with a fringe. And he is carrying quite a bit of luggage: two backpacks and a large suitcase. "I'm moving house, because I've just started a new job," he explains.

It took him fifty minutes by train to get from Dongguan (population 8.2 million) to Guangzhou (population 15 million), and from here it takes another hour by bus to reach Hecun, a suburb of Foshan (population 7.2 million). This part of Guangdong province is just right for people who enjoy seeing a lot of Chinese people crammed together in a very small space.

I ask Yangwei about his profile.

"In my last job, I had a lot of time to myself," he explains. "I just had to keep a WeChat website up to date. Nothing creative, just adding a new photo or text from time to time. So boring, oh my God." For days, he experimented with finding the best combination for his emoji figures. The lazy days are over now, though. Because the pay was so bad, he moved to the auto industry.

"I work for *Wolkse Wogon*. Heard of it?"

"No."

"It's a German company, I think."

"Oh, you mean Volkswagen? Of course I know them."

"The German share is only a small percentage. But for better sales, it's always good to say, 'Made in Germany.'"

"Do the cars sell well here?"

"I don't know. I'm still learning. At the moment, I just stand at the entrance and say, 'Hello' and 'Welcome.' Oh man, so boring." Repeatedly, he has to realign his glasses, which are slightly too loose and threaten to slip down his nose.

We get off the bus at a side street next to the highway. It is twenty-five minutes on foot from here to the center of Hecun. On the uneven paving Yangwei's trolley bag is having a contest with the rattle of trucks and the honking motorbikes to see which can make the most noise. To the left a much-too-wide road without markings, to the right cereal crops and greenhouses. It smells of building rubble, burnt plastic, rubber and glue—the fragrance could be called something like Accident at the Chemical Plant.

"You are the first tourist here, for sure," says Yangwei.

We turn into a street with brand-new but featureless five-story apartment blocks; the place gives the impression of recently having been enlarged considerably. I feel the people looking at me as I pass. I have often felt this in my travels, mostly in rural areas such as remote villages in Myanmar, Chechen mountain regions or Indonesian rain forests, places where foreigners seldom visit and where I must have seemed like someone from a different world. But here, everyone looks at me and the surroundings are not providing a plausible reason. It's a strange feeling to be on a freshly tarred street in the middle of a new housing estate and to still be thought of as utterly out of place.

Yangwei told me that he would be earning some 1,000 yuan (almost US$150) a month initially but more soon, he hoped. His rent for the apartment is 400 yuan (US$57) a month.

"My apartment is very small," he says. "We have to share a bed. Have you got a sleeping bag?"

"Yes."

I always travel with a light sleeping bag; it is, after my cell phone, my favorite piece of gear. After all, I never know what to expect from my lodgings.

Yangwei's apartment on the fifth floor is about two hundred square feet and consists mostly of a bedroom with a closet plus a tiny kitchenette. The only window opens to the neighboring brick wall a mere three feet away. The shower has an electric cable running along the wall, the state and placement of which would meet the requirements for the charge of attempted murder, and because of the lack of space, the squat toilet also acts as the drain. Everything is painted white, except the front door, which is made from a dark wood, and the bedcovers, which are pink and baby blue with a print of hearts and teddy bears.

Yangwei begins unpacking with great panache: electric kettle, hair dryer, pegs, clothes hangers; the Bible, a romance novel titled *Sahara*, the *Oxford Advanced Learner's Dictionary*; and then a black jacket with "SAIC Volkswagen" printed on it. Some German company or other with a small percentage share? Bull! This is the biggest of a number of VW alliances, with a fifty-fifty share model. For many years, that was the maximum

57

share granted in China to a foreign automotive business. The rules are now at last being changed, but still, the most lucrative automotive market in the world is only accessible with hefty concessions in coerced cooperation with local companies, including the transfer of know-how, of course. Time and again, foreign managers were astonished to discover almost identical copies of their own engine or chassis designs on the cars of their "partners."

"Give me a hug!" says Yangwei suddenly. "Welcome! I hug all my guests!"

Good, we now have that behind us.

For the evening meal we go to a corner restaurant run by members of the Islamic Hui minority. The walls have been papered with pictures of the delicacies on offer and I choose Lanzhou-style lamian noodles.

Yangwei, who seemed shy and insecure at first, appears to have gained confidence, and his flood of words can hardly be halted, almost as if all of a sudden everything that he usually holds back has to now come out. "Europeans think that the Chinese are fixated on work. This is unfair. You can be lazy, but we have to work like mad; otherwise, we'd be fired. There are always ten people who want your job."

A muscular waiter wearing a prayer cap brings steaming bowls of soup with handmade noodles and chunks of beef. He has tired eyes from working hard—his restaurant is open from 6 AM to 10 PM every day.

"I was in Serbia because it's easy to go there without a visa. Nobody smiles there. I was frightened nonstop that someone would pull out a gun and shoot me. Europeans are so cold. And lazy—in particular, the Italians, a friend told me, but in return, less cold."

"You can't make such generalizations," I try to interrupt him, but he's just getting into his stride.

"How do you make a European happy? Give him a beer and put him on a beach!" When Yangwei laughs it sounds like stringing together lots of "ch" sounds (as in cheese, not charisma). "Crazy. Why do you like beaches so much? They're totally boring."

His cell phone rings, so I can dedicate a bit of time to my soup without being exposed to further slights. What image of Europe will someone like Yangwei have in twenty or thirty years, when China will play a considerably greater role in world politics? How will such sentences sound when the speaker is absolutely convinced of his country's superiority? I don't have time to bring these thoughts to a conclusion, as three minutes later, his phone call ends.

"My mother. She said that I shouldn't sleep in the same room as you, and I shouldn't use any of your things, because Europeans have so many diseases from their unsound way of life, having sex everywhere with everyone. Are you diseased? Shall I bring you to a hospital and have you checked?"

He certainly sounds a bit worried now.

"Thanks, but it's not necessary. I feel fine."

That seems to satisfy him, and he changes the subject. "My foreign friends say that I absolutely must visit Berlin. It's in northern Germany, isn't it?"

"Northeast."

"Is it good there?"

"Yes, lots of creativity and culture, with historic places on every corner. You can learn a lot about the division of Germany and about the Nazi era there."

"You are not allowed to talk about that, are you?"

"About what?"

He lowers his voice as if we're conspiring and almost whispers the following words: "If the German government finds out that you are talking about Nazis, you will be arrested, won't you?"

"No. But it is forbidden to deny the mass murders at Auschwitz and to hoist a flag with a swastika in your yard."

"But last year some Chinese got into trouble in Germany because they talked about Nazis."

"What?"

"Yes, outside an old building. You say that you are allowed to do it, but if the Chinese do it, they get into trouble. So unfair." Yangwei appears seriously indignant but now speaks at a normal volume.

"What exactly did they do?"

"Let me check." He baidus the story on his cell phone. "Ah, they did the thing with their arms raised."

"The Nazi salute?"

"Yes."

"Oh God, yes, that is also illegal."

"How do you do a Nazi salute?"

"You stick out your right arm with the palm pointing downwards."

"Like this? Or a bit higher?"

"Yes, that's right, but you can lower your arm now."

"But it's right, isn't it? Is the angle right?"

"Yes, it is."

60 Satisfied, he sizes up the result from the tips of his fingers to his shoulder, as if trying to memorize the precise position.

"You really can..." I look around to see if anyone is watching us. Two guests at the next table hastily look down at their soup bowls. The surveillance camera on the ceiling continues filming silently.

"Okay," says Yangwei, finally lowering his arm. "So, in any case, the tourists took each other's picture in front of a kind of castle. Here."

The photo in the article is of the Reichstag, the German parliament building in Berlin.

"They were arrested, and each of them had to pay a five-hundred-euro [US$570] fine! For taking a few photos. Laws are so strict in Germany, I would be scared to travel there."

. . . .

BACK IN THE apartment Yangwei remembers that he only has one key. I offer to leave the house with him at 8:00 AM, when he has to go to work.

"No that's too early for you. You're an old man," he answers.

Nobody can so nonchalantly pack thoughtfulness, paternalism and indignity into one sentence like the Chinese. Later, he again displays a tendency towards unfiltered expression of opinion when looking through photos of my previous travels in my Couchsurfing profile. "You have changed completely. You used to be very handsome," is his comment.

We agree on my going downstairs with him in the morning to let him out with the key. Afterwards, I can return to the apartment and give my aged bones a rest (I'm fifteen years older than him).

He moves his trolley bag in front of the bathroom door because there are no hooks or shelves to put things on inside and drapes his clothes on it, and then disappears for a shower. 61

I thought that the lack of space was going to be the main problem during the night, but I didn't know anything about the midges then: a continuous whirring at the ears, in the ears, around the ears makes it impossible to think of sleeping. There isn't a Chinese saying that goes something like, "Ten midges are worse than five cats," but it is still true. Almost every ten seconds Yangwei snuffles noisily, which also doesn't sound like Mozart. Shortly after midnight, he turns on the light and we both go hunting insects. We get a couple but by no means all of them. Touchingly, he apologizes for the inconvenience, though he can't help it. The next day I feel old, darned old.

· · · · · · · · · ·

YANGWEI IS ALREADY in his work clothes: black jacket, crumpled white shirt and black patent-leather shoes. He shoulders an Adidas backpack with a thermos in one of the side pockets. When he walks, the dangling label from a tea bag looks like a little fluttering butterfly. I go downstairs with him and let him out. Men are surging out of other doors in identical black-and-white outfits, and women in pantsuits head west towards the dealerships with the shiny new cars. One of the crowd turns suddenly and runs towards to me. "I've forgotten my belt!" a stressed-out Yangwei announces, and runs back upstairs.

Then there is peace. I lie down on the bed again and doze a bit.

Afterwards, I commit myself once again to some digital self-optimization. This time I try out the extremely popular Chinese app MyIdol. Again I take a selfie. "Scanning face" appears on the screen, and a green line moves up and down my photo. The next steps are "Analyzing face," "Calculating 3-D structure" and "Computing texture." Ready. The program now has a 3-D animated model of my head. Automatically, my head is given a body in a black suit and a white shirt, the look resembling the armada of auto dealers outside. This is the starting point, and from here, I can do the optimizing.

There are countless options to beautify yourself: clothing, makeup, hats, shoes. I can embed my head in a huge hoodie with a print of a panda on it, dress like an emperor or give myself the body of a ballerina. In the end, I decide on a cap with a hamster on it and a red brocade blazer.

Now, I can let my clone appear in a ready-made animation film, get him to sing "Happy Birthday" in Chinese or make him a kung fu warrior, a pianist or a pole dancer. People who know the interactive website ElfYourself will have a rough idea of the possibilities, but MyIdol is light-years ahead technically. If more people outside of China knew of this free app, it would have millions of users. The provider is a company called Huanshi Ltd., about which there doesn't seem to be much precise information anywhere, except that they have three similar apps in their portfolio. I don't know who they are, but they have my face. I decide to think nothing bad of it and continue experimenting with funny hats and shoes. It's simply too much fun.

From: Qing Policewoman
Who is your host? Have you got a couch or a bed?

To: Qing Policewoman
Bed

To: Qing Policewoman
And no cats this time

63

From: Qing Policewoman
Good. I hope no one climbs onto you tonight

Back in the real world, the center of Hecun consists of one main street with restaurants and businesses: a China Mobile shop, a KTV karaoke bar and a bubble tea shop. Men wear their T-shirts high so that they sit comfortably on their rounded bellies, and they spit on the street—"kchouchchch," the sound of old China; the only things louder are the cars and trucks, whose horns, if you stand too close, cause tinnitus immediately. In some of the windows there are little Santa Claus figures and "Merry Christmas" banners. It is the beginning of April, but why remove them if they look nice? The Chinese New Year decorations are also usually left hanging for twelve months. I notice a surplus of barbershops, with a haircut costing fifteen yuan, less than three U.S. dollars.

A few streets farther on I come across a river that does a number of things, but flowing isn't one of them. It is a dark gray mass in which plastic bags and unwanted food packaging are floating and wrecks of old wooden boats are rotting. The air smells like burning coal, scratching the throat and irritating the eyes; there is too much industry in the surroundings. A healthy economy is more important to China than a healthy people; the state propaganda speaks of a necessary evil that simply comes with progress. Nevertheless, as the leaders realized that just carrying on would make a part of the country uninhabitable in a few decades, environmental technologies managed to be included in the next five-year plan. Today, there is no other country with as many solar plants and electric cars.

I leave the center of town and head towards the highway,
approaching the automotive companies. I discover shops for brands that I have never seen in Europe, their logos looking to me more like the emblems of an extraterrestrial fleet from some computer game: Cowin, Bisu, Sinotruk, Great Wall, FAW, Trumpchi.

Then I cross the highway using the pedestrian underpass leading to a huge site with international models.

When the first Volkswagen Santana left the production line of a factory in Shanghai in April 1983, cars were still mainly reserved for functionaries and cab drivers. Ordinary people rode bikes or motorbikes, or took the bus. If someone had said then that China would soon be the greatest sales market for cars in the world, people would have thought they were crazy. The unsophisticated Santana, a plain middle-class sedan with a notchback, was a flop in Europe but became a best seller in China, even though the horn was far too quiet for Far Eastern demands and the lack of comfort in the rear seat was criticized—driver and passenger seats were less important in China, as the owners usually sat in the back.

The VW managers showed foresight by backing early what was later to be a lucrative market. Still, mostly different models are successful here than in Europe, the model names sounding like a Brazilian Carnival song: "Lavida! Lamando! Santana Jetta Bora!"

The factory here in Foshan has just expanded. VW is banking on the future of electric cars and SUVs, and they will soon

65

be producing 600,000 instead of 300,000 cars per year. It is still less than the plant in Wolfsburg in Germany, but Foshan's is only one of nineteen vw factories in China. Nineteen car factories. The scale reflects how important this market has become.

And the Chinese adore successful companies. For instance, Yangwei's parents—it was their idea that their son sign on in Hecun, Yangwei tells me later over an after-work lemon tea on the main street.

"They couldn't care less whether I'm happy in my job. They only look at the money," he says. If things work out, he could be earning 10,000 yuan (almost us$1,500) a month thanks to sales bonuses. "Maybe in ten years' time I will thank them, but at the moment, they're just putting me under pressure," he grumbles.

Yangwei admits to having no idea about cars. He learned website design, he speaks good English and he has traveled to seven foreign countries and throughout half of China. But if he had to explain the difference between a station wagon and a coupé, he would have to pass. "On my second day, a customer asked me about the technical details of a car. I could only say, 'Sorry, sorry' and quickly grab a colleague."

In the first two months he is expected to mostly look over other people's shoulders and learn everything there is to know about cars, as well as the Rules for Sales Staff, a list of forty points that he has printed out and keeps in his pocket.

"'You need clean clothes and must always smile,'" he reads out to me. "Oh, man! This is so boring and stupid. I feel like a schoolkid."

In the tea shop is a little TV set showing a sitcom where a young man is meeting his prospective father-in-law for the first time. For some reason, which was probably explained earlier, he is wearing a pink tutu and is visibly embarrassed.

Yangwei translates a few other rules for me: "'Ask the customer his name and telephone number. After talking to him, you must contact him within twenty-four hours. Offer him a test drive and offer him soy vice.'"

"What?"

"You don't know what soy vice is?"

"No."

"S-E-R-V-I-C-E," he spells out.

"Aha! Service!"

"No, it's pronounced 'soy vice.' Wait, I'll check in a translation program. Oh, you're right. 'Service.' But here, this one's also great: 'Don't let the phone ring more than three times; at the most, eight seconds. Say: "Hello, what do you need, how can I help you?" Listen to the customer.'"

A small man in a polo shirt places some pink flyers for a massage parlor called Xiang Jiang on our table. The text promises "new feelings, new experiences" and, as a special offer, treatment for detoxifying the bladder. The need for toxins to be driven out of the body is a major topic in traditional Chinese medicine. The portraits of eight very young ladies, who, thanks to digital optimization, resemble bug-eyed extraterrestrials, suggest a kind of detoxification that cannot be found in medical textbooks. *Offer service:* the secret of a successful business.

"'Talk to the customers about an interesting topic to create a good atmosphere,'" Yangwei continues reading. "*That* I can't do; I'm much too shy. What am I supposed to talk about? Something like this here?"

He points to the flyer. On the back are printouts of a couple of discount coupons. "I could say, 'If you buy one of my cars, you will get a free *emperor massage*.' It's all such utter nonsense."

But he does see parallels between the two businesses—a colleague recently told him that the most important thing for a salesman is to look good. "Then you can sell them anything. Westerners have it much easier; they are attractive by nature."

"If that were true, then the customers would also be attractive, and then the salesman wouldn't be anything special."

"Also true. But in China, both are ugly. That's why it's difficult to communicate with customers. Both are thinking: *Why are you so ugly? Why are you talking to me?*"

"Oh, so that's why Chinese tourists completely buy out European luxury stores! Because of the beautiful sales staff."

"No, in that particular case the people don't care at all. The prices are much lower there."

The beautiful foreigner. One of the most striking impressions of a trip to China for many is a previously unknown feeling of attractiveness. Westerners are often complimented, by men and women equally. It is typical to hear a "Your Chinese is very good" when you splutter out a falsely accented *ni hao*, or praise for your chopstick skills when only one in three attempts actually reaches your mouth.

However, there is a real admiration hiding somewhere behind the flattery—the prevailing beauty ideal is "Western." The cosmetics industry and plastic surgery business profit considerably from promising white skin, narrow cheeks and big eyes.

68 Even the language reflects a certain admiration. In Mandarin, Americans, for instance, are called *meiguoren*, which translates to "beautiful people" (accordingly, the English are heroic people, Germans virtuous people and French law-abiding people.)

Because of their comparatively larger size, the average European woman in China feels like Helga the Viking, whereas foreign men suddenly find themselves two notches up on the attractiveness scale. In an astonishingly explicit article in the Chinese state newspaper the *Global Times*, a frustrated foreign woman complained about her sexual marginalization—her independence and strong opinions frightened off Chinese men. Other male foreigners were out of the question because once they gained a taste for "the amount of attention [they] get from Chinese women, with their slender and supple bodies and their compliance in bed, Caucasian women can no longer keep up."

Before 50 percent of readers start downloading visa applications, a short warning about the downside. Womanizers don't have a particularly good reputation, and the term LBH, or Loser Back Home, has become well established here, referring to the cliché *laowai* who back home just can't get his act together, in terms of both his job and his love life, but in China manages to get a spectacularly well-paid job as an English teacher and begins living the life of a rock star. A hip-hop song called "Stupid Foreigners" by Fat Shady from Chengdu shows little sympathy: "You're a loser in your own country—and come to China to be taken seriously" are two of the more innocent lines. The rest contains several repetitions of "fuck you," "clean my car" and "I'm gonna shoot you."

Back in Hamburg, Yang told me that they'll take on English teachers everywhere. This is not quite true anymore in the megacities, where they usually hire only native speakers with certificates. And, of course, there are excellent foreign teachers. But every now and then you come across a cheerful Colombian, Russian or Ukrainian who simply says they're from the U.S. or Canada and, despite a heavy accent and a limited

69

vocabulary, they are allowed to teach in schools. The demand is simply too great; even elementary students are driven to private English schools on the weekends by their middle-class helicopter parents.

I write to a host in Yangshuo, a city near Guilin famous for its cormorants-in-front-of-karst-cliffs photos. The man is head of a language institute for adults and has an unusual offer: visitors get free room and board if they take on two hours of one-on-one conversation practice per day. Sounds like it's time for the English teacher rock star life, so I agree.

The Best Chinglish Phrases

1 Be careful clothes sandwich (warning on an escalator)

2 Millet pepper love on small cock (on a menu in Shenzhen)

3 No professional doors (warning in an elevator)

4 The ss dental ministry of denture (at a dentist's office in Kashgar)

5 Alive steel rail don't climb over (warning on a mountain railway track in Zhangjiajie)

WILD WEST STREET

SAY GOOD-BYE TO Yangwei and take the bus on the highway to the airport-sized high-speed train station of Guangzhou. It consists of some 79,000 tons of steel and 530,000 tons of concrete, which is enough for twenty-eight platforms and a massive waiting hall.

After going through passport control and the luggage scanner, I wander around in the huge pillar-free waiting area. Passengers are only allowed on the platform shortly before departure. The design of the nose of these bullet trains, type CRH2, looks like a cross between Snoopy and a white dragon. The train starts a little before the announced departure time. Chinese high-speed trains always leave between fifteen and forty-five seconds early. This might be a very German observation, but once you start watching out for it, you notice it again and again.

Frantically, passengers seek out their spots. On each side of the aisle are two seats, with blue covers and a white cloth draped over the headrest. My neighbor, a woman of about forty, is on the telephone nonstop. She doesn't speak Mandarin but a local dialect and at a volume that is painful to the ears, though she's not even swearing. I record some of her conversation on my cell phone so I can get it translated later. She screams her arrival time and what she plans to cook later, as if it were the only sure way that her conversation partner could understand her all those miles away. A staff member walks through our train car and dusts around the passengers' feet.

China is railway country number one. Every minute, 10 million Chinese are on the tracks. Nowhere on the planet are there as many high-speed lines, and nowhere are there more plans for expansion. In the twenty-one years it took Germany to build a Munich–Berlin intercity rail link (400 miles), China laid 15,500 miles of high-speed track.

The onboard TV is also geared towards progress. They show the taikonauts in the Tiangong-2 space station 236 miles above the earth. China wants to send a probe to Mars soon and is planning a manned flight to the moon in 2024.

At least looking out the window the countryside is like a photo book from the seventies—tree-covered karst cliffs in the mist, uncountable numbers of them, like giant green camel humps that jut out of the landscape, a softer and more rounded counter-design to the angular high-rises a couple of miles away. Different epochs seem to clash when a train from the future hurtles through the lands of the past. A good two hours later, when I disembark in Yangshuo, the station is the most modern building far and wide, with nature all around white houses of four stories at the most.

The way to the bus stop is an ordeal, with men with cigarettes behind their ears shouting, "Taxi, mister! Where are you going?" "Hotel, hotel!" or "Taxi, hotel, lady!" I feel as if I'm at an auction. The brashest of them grabs me by the arm and with "No bus, no bus" tries to persuade me that the longish vehicle twenty yards away is just a hallucination. Luckily, I trust my senses more than his propaganda, and soon a clean bus takes me downtown for very little money.

The Zhouyue English College is another three miles outside the city. A chain-smoking motorbike cab driver, whose relationship to traffic regulations is improvisational, gets me there via the sidewalk, red lights, pedestrian crossings and, occasionally, in the midst of oncoming traffic.

The school director ("You will never be able to remember my Chinese name, so just call me Frank") greets me in a kind of lobby, wearing a gray sweater, sneakers and black horn-rimmed glasses. On the wall are the teachers' university certificates; almost half of them studied something to do with languages, but philosophy and business administration are also well represented.

73

"You have two individual lessons between 6:30 and 8:30 PM each day," says Frank. "It's simply about speaking a lot." He makes a copy of my passport and visa for the authorities, then leads me to the living quarters on the other side of the road.

My room on the sixth floor with two wooden bunk beds reminds me of a hostel dormitory, but at the moment, I'm the sole guest. Next to the room is a rooftop terrace with washing lines and a view of white village houses and green karst cliffs.

I have my first evening free, so I hire a bright red e-scooter and breeze silently to the center of Yangshuo. The scooter is a bit too small, so I constantly bang my knees. At night, I have to charge the battery for a couple of hours, as a full load is enough for around forty miles. Does anyone understand why in eco-conscious European cities so many scooters still run on gas?

On every corner in Yangshuo there are bike rental stores. Recently, one of the large national suppliers of public rental bikes wanted a piece of the cake, which incensed the local dealers to such an extent that they threw quite a number of the interloper's bikes into the Li River. The business moved elsewhere.

At the beginning of the famous West Street, I stop to immerse myself in the stream of people moving along the cobblestones. Behind a tour guide holding a red flag and a loudspeaker on a lanyard, a group of Chinese tourists marches on like a moderately well-disciplined trailblazing force, with selfie sticks at the ready, always prepared to shoot objects or creatures that could look good behind or next to their own likeness.

The purpose of security camera–lined West Street is to provide these visitors with as many background motifs as possible while also wringing as much money out of them as possible for snack stands, hotels and bars. Tour operators in traditional silk costumes advertise "Bamboo, bamboo"—boat tours on bamboo rafts. And souvenirs, souvenirs, souvenirs. I wonder whether, in the course of their travels, it dawns on some of the tourists, on viewing the group outfit daily, that maybe the free cap and backpack with the travel company logo are not quite the awesome goodies they thought them to be when making the booking.

There are plenty of streets of this kind in China, and they all look remarkably similar. The standard fare is: Kentucky Fried Chicken, a drum and ukulele store, a T-shirt printing service, a store for combs made out of antlers, a virtual reality simulator store and a fast-food restaurant courting racist guests with the slogan "We don't serve Japanese." Additionally, in Yangshuo there are a conspicuous number of bars selling German beer or bratwurst. And there are a number of bars with dancers wearing very little and entertaining a mostly male audience that waves snake-shaped balloons to pop music. R-rated entertainment meets a kid's birthday party. Is there a sadder sight than middle-aged men conducting the song "Despacito" with orange, sausage-shaped balloons, always slightly out of sync, while clasping bottles of overpriced Tsingtao beer and staring bashfully at the hips of a bunny-eared beauty? Some of them wave plastic sticks with two plastic hands fixed at the top

75

that make a clacking sound. The ignominious gimmicks are handed out by the bar staff and accepted gratefully—hurrah, freebies.

Outside, twenty policemen dressed in black with anti-riot helmets and batons look like sinister counterparts to the tourist groups, like a black shadow following them. Nothing should get out of hand on Wild West Street. I return to the e-scooter and head back to school.

· · · · · · · · · ·

CLASSROOM 301 HAS a grated window, a couple of chairs arranged around a table, on the blackboard a few words from the previous lesson: "career," "fulfillment" and "trade." Here, I meet a few English students in the following days. They spend nine months here and at the end of the course receive a certificate. During our conversations I learn a lot about everyday life in China, about their career plans and about earning money. The main topics are business in the past and business in the future, the transitory nature of profit and the necessity of flexibility in order to remain successful.

Lisa, twenty-seven, sold bras for her mother's company, and then went on to open with her sister a nail care studio that initially brought in a lot of money, until five other nail studios opened on the same street and the business was no longer worthwhile. She's now considering joining her cousin's travel agency, but business isn't so good anymore because everyone is booking on the internet.

Rooney, thirty-one, worked for eight years building engines for General Motors but is unsure about the future because of Donald Trump; growth cannot continue as it is now and exports to the USA will probably take a nose dive.

76

Win, nineteen, worked in a cutlery and tableware store, six days a week, up to twelve hours a day, but dreams of working abroad, possibly in Thailand as a tour guide. During these conversations I sense a considerable difference in mentality between Europeans and the Chinese. Europeans have an almost tangible fear of change, a romantic notion that, to a large extent, things should carry on just as they are. In China, however, change is accepted as a natural state you must adapt to; life is a continuous construction site, and "arriving" is not envisaged.

During the day, I explore the countryside on the e-scooter. The karst hillocks in the silvery morning mists seem almost magical, like gigantic sleeping ghosts draped in green. The cormorant fishermen from the famous photos, however, only exist in a folklore show, as one of many entertainment options including a stunt car circus, water caves/mud baths and a "20-Yuan-Banknote-Photo" outing (the banknote shows a particularly idyllic spot on Li River). On some stretches of the river there are traffic jams when too many bamboo rafts are in use all at once. The locals have weather-beaten faces of the healthy color Chinese city dwellers try to avoid by using bucketloads of skin whitener because they don't want to appear "poor."

A French engineer named Sébastien becomes my roommate. "You like schools? Then I have an idea for you," he says, and tells me about a Couchsurfing host in a village called Wenshi, just a few hours from here. "Charley—crazy guy but really nice. He's in his mid-thirties and an English teacher and was also teaching here in Yangshuo until recently. Here are his contact details. I'll write him that you might contact him. He'll take you on for sure." And sure enough, a message soon arrives.

77

From: Charley
Warmly welcome! I will be happy to meet you!

To: Charley
Thanks, I'm also looking forward to meeting you!

From: Charley
You're a friend of Seb's, so you're also a friend of mine.
Could I listen to your voice?

Via WeChat, I send him a short greeting as a voice message.
"Stee-phen! What are your hobbies? Things that you like doing, hobbies?" comes back, also as a sound recording. His voice is unusually high-pitched and nasal, and he enunciates every syllable of the English words precisely, like on a language course CD for beginners.

"Travel, books, playing guitar," I write, and it feels a bit as if I'm filling in an online dating profile.

He answers with another voice message: "Wow, that sounds great. But I think you could try to speak it out, not type it out."

"Okay, from now on I will answer with voice messages," I reply by text.

"Do you know why I want you to speak it out? Because I want to get used to your voice, your intonation. That's why."

A short while later, the next message from him arrives: "Do you sleep with Seb?" Whereas he has to get used to my intonation, I have to get used to his word choice.

"We share a room, yes. He's sitting next to me." Sébastien sends a "Hello, Charley" towards my cell mic.

"Good night, Stee-phen. You're a friend of Seb's, so you're also a friend of mine," he repeats.

DOGS AND
LOCAL POLITICS

THE MOTORBIKE TAXI takes me to a bus, the bus to Guilin station, then a cab to Guilin West station and from there another bus to Wenshi. It is always more complicated to travel from a large place to a smaller one than the other way around, and here my main problem is the local dialect. People don't understand me when I say "Wenshi" because they pronounce it "Wen-si." It is no less tricky with numbers, because *shi* (ten) sounds like *si* (four) in the local dialect. As if the subtle pronunciation differences of Chinese sibilants were not challenging enough.

After the decrepit Yutong bus has optimistically spent fifty minutes combing the city in the hope of finding further passengers on some obscure corner, it finally heads for the highway going east. The farther we travel from the city, the shorter the houses become and the taller the surrounding green hillocks. The wheels rumble, knotted plastic drapes flap against the windows and, from the seat behind me, I hear the sounds of some trendy smartphone video game: clinking money and a woman's voice that keeps saying, "Great!" accompanied by a marimba triad.

From my seat, which is in need of a thorough cleaning, I watch greenhouses and red Sinopec gas stations flash by—"Great!"—little cloudy gray lakes and brown rivers— "Great!"—and regularly in the small villages, shop owners taking a midday nap on their counters—"Great!" The jingle of coins. Doo-da-loo.

Everyone on the bus has internet access except for the person who needs it most—me. Up to now I've neglected getting a Chinese SIM card, out of sheer laziness, actually, but I manage to convince myself that it is a rational decision, as it is more difficult to locate me without one. There is always a little bit of paranoia in a surveillance state. I pay my home network provider €1.99 for twenty-four-hour roaming, but it doesn't work. I've been traveling since morning, and Charley doesn't know when I am due to arrive. Without the internet in China, I'm an oddball without friends. "Great!" Doo-da-loo.

After two hours, the bus stops at the terminal in Wenshi. My cell phone displays a number of password-protected networks, some of the names consisting mainly of special symbols that don't inspire much confidence. Still, I try them out using "88888888" and "123456789" as passwords—without success. I walk down the main street, but there are no restaurants to be seen that could possibly have internet access, just a bank, general stores and a suntanned street trader selling large chunks of pork.

I go back to the bus station and ask a woman at the counter where I can find Wi-Fi.

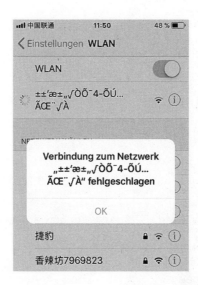

"*Mei you*—there isn't any," she says, her voice distorted through the mic behind the pane. I ask her whether she could write a WeChat message for me. Instead, she rummages for her phone and shows me an app called Wanle Jaoshi (meaning "strong key") that enables you to access many secure networks, at least for a short while. Spy technology for everyone. She asks me whether I have it. Sadly, no.

A customer in a red jacket offers to call my host if I have the number. I only have his WeChat contact details, but that doesn't help, as she is the first person I have met in China without a smartphone, just an old-fashioned flip phone.

The bus lady has another idea. She points to a phone store on the other side of the street. I walk over and find a range of models by internationally unknown companies like Hero Tod, Redgee, F-Fook and Coobe. I am just about to buy a Hero Tod phone, simply because of the sensational name, when the sales assistant takes my cell and logs me in to a Wi-Fi network.

81

From: Charley
Where are you now?

From: Charley
Stephan?

From: Charley
Why aren't you on time?

To: Charley
Really sorry, I had no internet. I'm now at Wenshi
bus station

From: Charley
Wenshi bus stop? Wait for me there

Back at the bus station I thank the lady at the counter. A
few minutes later, Charley arrives on his e-scooter with a pink
plastic roof. He is wearing suit pants, an orange sports jacket
and very thick glasses on a very round face.

"My parents are very happy to meet you," says Charley.
"They've specially killed the dog for you."

There's a short pause while I absorb the shock. Maybe he's
just joking.

"That really wasn't necessary," I then say. I have never meant
the sentence more. From a side street I hear the banging of
fireworks.

82   "It's a special day. Welcome! Take a seat!"

I squeeze behind him beneath the plastic rain covering.
Because of lack of space I have to sit slightly crookedly with
my backpack so as to not bang my head, my legs sticking up
like a grasshopper's.

"I've told my parents you are Stee-phen, my old friend from Germany," he says. "I've told them you're very polite and very talkative. Because you're a friend of Seb's, you're also a friend of mine. Maybe it's better not to mention couchsurfing, because it might be strange for them. Do you understand?"

The village consists of a series of dismal concrete detached houses with stores selling bits and pieces on the ground floor and living quarters above. On each entrance there are red-and-gold images of the door gods Yuchi Gong and Qin Qiong, two warriors from the Tang dynasty in the seventh century. With beards in full flow and terrifying halberds, they are supposed to ward off evil spirits. Often hanging next to them are cartoons of happy dogs with saucer eyes from the New Year celebrations; after all, 2018 is the Year of the Dog. Some of them have tongues sticking out as if to mock me.

Charley turns into a side street with plenty of potholes. Instead of slowing down before them, he just shouts: "Be careful!"

We pass through a gateway into the yard of his parents' house—or rather, two houses. On the right, there is a dilapidated old stone structure with traditional roof shingles, and on the left, a new three-story concrete building with yellow walls. Two red lanterns decorate the new house's main entrance, which leads directly to the living room. A mother hen and chicks are pecking at corn in the inner courtyard.

Charley introduces his parents. His father is an electrician, a stout man with a high forehead and brown skin. He holds a Zhenlong cigarette up to my face; the Chinese always offer a cigarette when they want to smoke. Thanking him, I decline. Charley's mother has gray hair and plenty of laugh lines; to welcome me, she presses a handful of ultra-sweet candy and peanuts into my hand. She then disappears

83

towards the kitchen. I try not to imagine what she might be doing there.

"Maybe you want to take a look at my school—then we have to go now," urges Charley.

I quickly take my backpack to the first floor, where a room with a freshly made king-size bed has been prepared. The decorations on the wall in the anteroom are sensational: a propaganda picture of Xi Jinping and his wife next to a bullet train hangs nearby a huge photo of naked twin babies, a kind of lucky charm that is supposed to bestow on the people living here plenty of offspring. The highest authority in the state hangs on one wall and the most helpless beings in the country on the other, and everyone entering the room is somewhere between in the pecking order.

At regular intervals, red rectangles the size of CD cases are stuck to closet doors, walls and windows, rather like the tags left by debt collectors in preparation to auction off your possessions, though these rectangles are actually meant to bring good luck. The living room on the ground floor is guarded by a larger-than-life portrait of Mao on the wall tiles. He looks on seriously but kindly, his dark gray collar tightly buttoned, the outline of his head highlighted in white like a halo. Next to him are children's and grandchildren's school reports and certificates, as if they're offerings to the former supreme leader.

On the scooter, with plenty of "Be careful" warnings from Charley, we hurtle off towards the school. Again, we pass several doors with New Year decorations showing happy dogs.

"What kind of dog was it, then?" I ask.

"A normal dog. My parents are a little sad about it, but we wanted to show you how hospitable we are."

"It's... a great honor. But I feel sorry for the normal dog!"

"He wasn't a pet. He just lived here for nine months and guarded the house. He was called Xiao Bai, Little White One."

I'm about to start a discussion of the meaning of the word "pet," but he changes the topic.

"There are forty-seven kids in the class and they are already very curious about you," he shouts into the wind. "Maybe you could start by telling them about the methods used in learning English in your country. Then you could go on to ask them about the scenic spots in this region. It's important to motivate them to learn English. Many of them are not all that good."

The school is enclosed by a wall and consists of a number of elongated buildings resembling army barracks. There is a basketball court and a soccer pitch, a hall of residence and a four-story main building with red lettering reading: "Education is the national plan, education brings prosperity to the people."

Elm trees line the path to the schoolyard, and the whole complex looks clean and modern with a capacity for some thousand pupils. Charley leads me to a classroom. We enter to applause, forty-seven pairs of sixth-grader eyes looking towards me expectantly. On the desks are heaps of books and notepads.

My grasp of the language is enough for a short introduction in Mandarin: "*Ni hao, wo jiao Stephan. Wo shi deguo ren. Renshi nimen wo hen gaoxing!*—Hi, my name is Stephan. I come from Germany. I'm pleased to meet you!"

The audience cheers. Curious onlookers are gathered at a grated window in the adjoining hall, and I feel like a rock star. From now on, I'll speak in English. Which topics had Charley suggested? I've forgotten. Never mind, I'll just explain why English is so important in my country, that I write books, that I like China and that I've been to many countries.

"Stee-phen! I have a suggestion—maybe you could talk a little slower," says Charley in his inimitable way. "Maybe" seems to be his favorite English word.

So I speak more slowly; nevertheless, he translates some terms. The job title "writer" he puts on the blackboard. If the kids become too loud he makes a "time-out" sign with two flat hands, like a volleyball coach. Sometimes he questions them to see if they have understood me, and in unison they all shout the answer. Towards the end of the lesson, the kids are allowed to ask me questions, which they do with earsplitting enthusiasm.

"Why are you so tall?" "How much do you earn?" "Have you got a girlfriend?" "What kinds of food do you like?" "What is your favorite animal?" "Can you use chopsticks?" (Much applause when I reply yes.) "Do you like flowers?" "Can you swim?" "Have you tried ginger tea?" "Can I shake your hand?"

Charley translates the most difficult question for me: "The girl at the front wants to know what you think of me, since we've known each other for years," he fibs.

Now a bit of diplomatic improvisation is required. "Charley is friendly, clever and good to talk to, very interesting."

"Did you understand that?" he asks, contentedly rubbing his palms together.

"Meiii youuu—noooo!" is the reply from almost forty-seven throats.

"Repeat it slowly, please," he says to me.

"Friendly, clever, good to talk to. Interesting," I say, as slowly as I can.

This time, they seem to understand, as after every attribute a number of them cheer, with the rest joining in immediately after. Party time in Wenshi junior high.

Suddenly, slightly distorted Big Ben chimes can be heard out of the PA system. The lesson is over. A couple of souvenir photos taken by plenty of cell phones and much screaming are unavoidable, and then Charley, grinning like the Cheshire cat, guides me towards the staffroom.

"They liked it a lot. Maybe you can do another lesson?" he asks.

"Of course," I reply.

He has a short conversation with one of his female colleagues, who seems to be his boss. Her answer sounds serious, almost like a reprimand.

Charley comes back to me: "They have a lot of homework to do now. We can go home." I suspect this is an excuse, and that she is actually worried about the noise and chaos another English class would cause.

"Going home," unfortunately, also means supper. I have just enough time to type "normal dog" into Google and click on images (my VPN access is working perfectly). The results? Shattering. Maybe I should try "little white dog"? Even worse.

The dining room is in the old house, a grim, smoky room with a fireplace. On entering, I bang my head against some chunks of meat hanging from the rafters to smoke. Sitting on tiny kindergarten-sized wooden stools around the fireplace are Charley's mother and father; Charley; his brother, who is a professional soldier; and his sister, with her seven-year-old daughter. The remains of Xiao Bai, already chopped into bite-sized pieces, are simmering in a dented jet-black wok.

I'm not a vegetarian and believe, in theory, that if people choose to eat meat, then from a moral viewpoint, it makes no difference whether what's put on the table is pig, rabbit or salamander, as long as it's not an endangered species. Other than that, it seems to me the distinction between the animal we prefer to stroke or eat or find disgusting is purely a matter of discretion. Cats and canaries—definitely not. Jellyfish and locusts—yuck. Turtles, no, but octopus and crabs and even suckling pig—of course you can eat them. Rabbit? Delicious. Hamster? For God's sake! Any extraterrestrial is guaranteed to have a completely different ranking.

Dogs, however, are not a usual item on the menu throughout China but can be found on tables in some of the southern regions. I have met many Chinese who have never eaten dog.

So much for my morality theory. In practice, I sit in front of this stew with leeks and tomatoes and wish I were somewhere far, far away. I can't help thinking about how dogs can build strong emotional connections to humans.

"Chi ba, chi ba," says Charley's mother, "Eat, eat."

Refusal is out of the question; this feast is, after all, in my honor. These people mean well, but I feel decidedly queasy—which is actually quite absurd, as there is almost nothing I like more when traveling than visiting places just like this smoky dining room where time appears to have stood still for fifty or eighty years. With my chopsticks, I transfer a couple of chunks of meat to the plate in front of me, while Charley's dad pours out homemade millet wine.

My first piece of meat is a bit of liver. What a way to start.

Survival strategy for eating dog, number one: chew with as little tongue contact as possible so as to be spared the taste. Success: moderate.

The next pieces are not offal, but they do contain a number of bones and some large chunks of fat. Poor old Xiao Bai tastes like a cross between beef and pork but somewhat richer. All around me, the family are merrily eating with gusto.

Survival strategy for eating dog, number two: let the piece of meat between your chopsticks cool off longer than necessary, and after swallowing, continue chewing to win time. Success: "Eat more," Charley insists.

Luckily, a bowl of radishes goes around, and I help myself so generously that anyone would think that I'm the greatest radish fan on the planet.

The conversations at the table pass me by; I can't follow it all with my little bit of Chinese, and anyway, I'm busy with my guilty conscience. If I weren't here, the dog would still be alive. I can forget about putting a note in this book, saying: "During my research no harm was done to any living creature."

Charley's father asks in my direction whether there are really so many thieves in France.

"He comes from Germany," answers Charley for me.

"Do you know that China has a very long cultural history?" his father asks.

"Yes, I've read books about it. Five thousand years," I reply, and he nods contentedly.

On a side table is a rice cooker, but on festive occasions rice is eaten at the end of a meal. Who an earth dreamt up that rubbish? After what feels like an eternity, Charley is the first to help himself to a portion.

"Oh, could I also have a bowl?" I ask.

"Have more meat first," he says generously, as rice is considered an uninteresting side dish, just there to fill you up when the real delicacies have been eaten.

"At the moment, I really feel like some rice," I say.

"There's still so much meat left," says Charley.

Survival strategy for eating dog, number three: use the sentence, "I love eating meat with lots of rice." Success: at last, the host is convinced. Charley gets up and serves me a bowl.

After a lot of wine and a lot of "eat more"s, I've finally managed to finish. I'm allowed to leave, passing Mao on the ground floor and Xi on the first floor, as if I only have to walk upstairs to rejoin the twenty-first century. Before falling asleep, I think of the dog, the millet wine and the smoky dining room. I would never have expected China to be *that* Chinese.

· · · · · · · · · ·

THE NEXT DAY, my crash course in rural family life in China continues. At breakfast, I sit beneath an image of the supreme leader with Charley's brother and parents; initially, Charley isn't there. An electric heater is mounted beneath the table to keep our feet warm, and on the table are peanuts, crackers and apples. Charley's brother has balanced his cell phone on top of a snack bowl, where it is showing a war film.

"Chi ba," says Charley's mom, pressing a hot yellowish clump of dough with a jellylike consistency into my hand. It is so hot that I have to keep juggling it from one hand to the other; there are no plates. With the words "He cha"—"drink tea"—she serves a ginger tea that is so scalding that I cannot drink it without a grimace. The taste makes me think of medicine—or something you'd use for an exorcism.

At least the clump of dough tastes good, something like corn, rice pudding and sugar. I hold it in my left hand and the exorcism tea in my right hand, while Charley's mother waves a plastic bag full of sour bits of seaweed in chili sauce in front of my nose, disappointed that I don't have a third arm to try them with.

"Chi ba! Chi ba! He cha!" is the chant of well-meant force-feeding—hospitality as the loss of personal liberty.

I stuff down bits of seaweed, crackers, peanuts and gummy candy—sour, salty, sweet, spicy, all on top of one another. There is no way I'm going to be defeated by breakfast. On the cell phone screen, brave soldiers shoot a couple of bad guys as Mao gazes wisely into the distance and Charley's mom tops up my ginger tea.

91

Charley joins us, sits on a plastic stool, belches audibly and says, "Eat, eat." Every half second that I don't actually eat something results in a reprimand. His mother informs him of my breakfast performance so far, with my initial declining of the chili seaweed probably playing a considerable role.

"You don't like our food?" Charley asks. He sounds seriously disappointed.

"I already ate lots before you came."

"You're not used to Chinese food, are you?"

"I've had more for breakfast than you."

"Too bad you don't like it."

. . . .

CHARLEY SAYS GOOD-BYE, as he has to go to the school. A tour of the town with his parents has been planned for me. His father tells me that he smokes three packs a day, coughing heavily to show he isn't exaggerating. "You are very tall. I am short. It's great that it's not raining today. Wenshi has thirty thousand inhabitants." The conversation doesn't advance; the language barrier is too large. Whenever I say half a sentence or just one word in broken Chinese, Charley's mother repeats what I have said and chuckles merrily.

Me: "*Wo de zhongwen bu tai hao.*" (My Chinese is not very good.)

She: "*Wo de zhongwen bu tai hao!*" Chuckle.

Me: "*Ni hao.*" (Hi.)

She: "*Ni hao!*" Chuckle.

Me: "*Xiexie.*" (Thanks.)

She: "*Xiexie!*" Chuckle.

I love our conversation.

In the market hall in the town center, in addition to selling fruit and vegetables, they also offer live geese and chickens, which flutter around in cages piled on top of one another. The uppermost has a wooden board on it that serves as a chopping board and a presentation platform for already slaughtered animals. The first two levels are for the living, the top level is for those about to die and the cages are constantly shaking from the blows of the cleaver. At a couple of other stalls, live cats and dogs can be bought, probably not as pets. It smells of feathers and raw meat. Somewhere, a firework explodes.

Charley's mother buys a live fish, which is passed to her in a plastic bag full of water, and a live chicken, which is transported in a jute bag. It would save on refrigeration costs worldwide if all markets sold fresh meat in this way, but of course most Western households aren't expected to do the slaughtering later. Does a chicken suffer more in a Chinese small town than at a huge European or North American slaughterhouse? I doubt it.

Customers can pay at every market stall by cell phone with WeChat; even the lady selling mushrooms at the roadside has a laminated sheet of paper with the necessary QR code. As further evidence of their town's progress, the parents take me to a brand-new supermarket, with softly humming air conditioning and calming music, selling kids' toys and bed linen, dish soap and pigs' heads and dozens of kinds of nuts and dried fruits. Two of the cashiers ask for a souvenir photo with me and I'm happy to comply.

On the way home we pass a poster of Xi Jinping that lists the twelve core socialist values: prosperity, democracy, civility, harmony, freedom, equality, justice, rule of law, patriotism, dedication, integrity and friendship.

93

"Who is the German head of state?" asks Charley's father.

"Angela Merkel."

"Have you got any German money? What is ten yuan?"

I dig a one-euro coin and a fifty-cent piece out of my pocket.

"This one is eight yuan, and this is four." I give them both to him.

We pass a number of quarries, the most important industry in the region. Six-foot water-cooled saw blades are processing boulders into classy flooring.

And we keep passing doors with cute dog pictures. "Xiao Bai," I say sadly, more to myself than my escort.

"Xiao Bai," echoes the mother, and chuckles.

· · · · · · · · ·

THE NEXT DAY, Charley has a day off school and takes me on a trip to the nearest large city. Bus number 6—a yellow, battery-driven vehicle—takes us to Guanyang. We drive through the hilly countryside and pass memorials to the Second Sino-Japanese War.

Charley sings a song in English in a whisper, "I just want to say, 'How are you?' You are so important in my heart."

"What are you singing?" I ask.

"A song that I've just made up for you."

During a short tour of the city, three things stand out: First, a KFC copy, which according to the sign outside is called MKC, but the cardboard menu says VFC—as long as there is a C at the end, it doesn't seem to matter. Second, the graphic pictures of pus-filled eczema wounds in the reception area of a hospital that we enter while searching for a bathroom. A few feet away there is a cutesy cartoon of sex workers and doctors that warns of the dangers of HIV infection. And, third, a private English school where a pushy receptionist invites me to take a look at a class. There, he snaps a whole lot of photos.

"I think they want to use them for their brochure," explains Charley. "If the school can claim to have foreign teachers, more people apply for courses."

I hope they send me a copy.

Charley's grandma lives on a side street and owns a tiny general store. She greets him by pinching his cheeks and asking him when he is finally going to introduce a wife to her. Steadily, I am getting to know more and more family members between two and seventy years old. One of them is Charley's uncle Yang, a retired senior official with the local authorities who was mainly responsible for religious affairs. His expensive check shirt and coal-black Luxgen U6 Turbo Eco Hyper SUV with tinted windows indicate his high status. With his suit pants sitting somewhat too high, he wears a belt with a silver buckle engraved with a lion.

"He wants to show us some of the local sights," says Charley. "Pretty places nearby, understand?" He has a highly irritating habit of saying everything twice with different words.

And then we are sitting in the huge SUV and the politician uncle turns on the stereo. Aggressive electro house beats thunder from the speakers, an unusual taste in music for someone

95

his age. He pulls up in front of a country house and, with large strides, leads the way across a rice field. We have to take off our shoes to cross a stream barefoot before reaching a cave entrance, which, to be honest, isn't the most spectacular of its kind. After one souvenir photo with the ex–local councillor, we return to the car. At the next stop, in a suburb called Renshi-cun, a path supposedly leads to a special rock. Unfortunately, we can't find the rock. Still, we manage a further group shot on a bridge over a filthy river.

"Do you know why my uncle is showing you this place?" asks Charley.

"No."

"He wants you to write in your book what a highly interesting place Guanyang is, understand?"

"Ah, I see."

Dear readers, Guanyang is highly interesting.

"Incidentally, he is also a writer—you are kind of colleagues. Maybe you could speak about it over the meal."

We drive back to grandma's apartment, where all sorts of delicacies are bubbling away on an electric stove. Other friends of the family drop by and we sit on tiny stools around the table—only the men; the women will get something to eat later.

"Okay, I now want to ask you a question, Stee-phen," Charley announces. "You only see men at the table. Do you know the reason?"

"No."

"The first reason is because there aren't enough stools. The second reason is that the women want to show respect."

"I would prefer a mixed table."

"Sadly, there aren't enough stools."

Bottles of Liquan 1998 lager do the rounds, and the three men opposite me, all around thirty, toast me constantly. Drinking alone is not done; either everyone drinks or no one. The Chinese toast by clinking the necks of bottles, not the bodies.

To accompany the drinks there is *kourou*, a delicious dish of taro and pork belly, and a huge pot with pieces of tofu and chicken—every part of it, including claws, heart and head.

"Drink up! Have another beer!" says Charley, while Uncle Yang fetches some documents in a transparent folder and begins noting something down with a pen.

"He is also working on a book, about the poet Liu Zongyuan."

Liu lived during the Tang dynasty in the eighth and ninth centuries and was a politician and poet who created works with titles like "The Song of the Caged Goshawk," "Dwelling by a Stream" and "River Snow." After an initially successful career in the civil service, he fell out of favor with the emperor by joining a reform movement, which criticized the unfair awarding of posts at the emperor's court, among other things. So he was an early fighter against corruption.

"What is the book about?" I ask, and Charley translates for his uncle.

There follows a two-minute lecture by the ex-politician.

"It's difficult to translate," says my host.

"Could you perhaps try to summarize it in a few sentences?"

"It's about Liu Zongyuan, the poet, and the person."

"Can't you tell me more?"

"Maybe later. Drink another beer."

The uncle pushes a handwritten document, a blank sheet of paper and a pen towards me. "He wants you to translate the text into German," says Charley.

"What does it say in Chinese?"

97

"It says: 'The experts and the learned have proven, and everyone in the city of Guilin knows, that Liu Zongyuan lived for a while in Guilin. My research comes to the same conclusion.' Maybe you could add the date and your signature below."

For a few moments I'm utterly speechless, something that seldom occurs.

"But… I haven't got the foggiest idea whether Liu Zongyuan lived in Guilin."

"It's not so important. It's just a small favor. Want some more *kourou*?"

I consider whether I should open a debate on academic integrity, but that would be doomed: first, because of Charley's lack of translating skills, and second, because it might disturb the friendly atmosphere. The uncle looks at me and at the pen in my hand. He is probably trying to apply the methodology of regional politics to book writing. Okay, let's go.

I jiggle the text a bit: "I don't know what the experts and the learned and the people of Guilin think about Liu Zongyuan. My research on him has yet to begin." Below I write the date and my signature.

"Thanks," says Charley. He takes the original Chinese document and draws three characters beneath it.

"What are you doing?" I ask.

"Just signing for you, with *Si Di Fen*. That's how your name would be written in Chinese."

Never try to be smarter than a canny local politician. With a satisfied smile, Uncle Yang puts both documents in his plastic folder.

"My uncle is offering to drive us home," says Charley.

I drink up the last drop of beer and notice for the first time the unusual label. There is a signature and a sentence of incorrect English: "With thanks for acting a good example! Bill Clinton, Former US President, July 1998." Whatever it is supposed to mean, I have some doubts about the authenticity of the quotation.

Unlike the following quotation, which I can vouch for: "You should pack your backpack. Get your things together and pack them. It's very important," says Charley, once we are home again. The next day I have to take an early bus so the advice is well meant. "Otherwise, you will have to do it tomorrow morning, and you will forget something in the rush. Understand? Better to pack everything now."

We are sitting again beneath the Mao tiles and nibbling nuts. The tube TV screen with a greenish tint is showing a historical war movie, featuring men with pigtails and long beards and plenty of screaming. Charley's mother forces more snacks and ginger tea on us with a big smile—*chi ba* and *he cha*—and just as I realize that I will miss Charley and his family, he suddenly becomes serious. He tells me of his worries about finding a wife—he is thirty-six—and bemoans his decision to return to the countryside. It was what his family wanted, and he obeyed, but he misses the modern world of Yangshuo and his job there.

"What do you think of me?" he asks suddenly. There again comes the Chinese fondness for ratings.

"I admire your work at the school. I think you put a lot of passion into teaching."

"And what else?"

"You are very friendly and an exceptional host."

"Thanks. The first thing I think about you is that you are good-looking. And second, you seem knowledgeable."

"Very nice of you."

"Will we appear in your book?"

"For sure."

"Great. My parents will be very happy to hear that."

ZHANGJIAJIE
Population: 1.5 million
Province: Hunan

VERY FAMOUS SOON

AFTER MANY HOURS on various buses, I reach Zhangjiajie
station in Hunan province. I have some time to spare here,
so at last I buy a Chinese SIM card and sit in a café to look for
potential hosts online. The waitress serves a drink that calls
itself cappuccino but consists of instant coffee powder, lots
of sugar and lukewarm milk. Maybe I should have gone to the
McCafé next door, but I was frightened off by a picture of their
bratwurst hamburger.

Zhangjiajie is a so-called fifth-tier city, despite a population
of 1.5 million and a famous national park nearby. The fifth tier
is the lowest category in a ranking system that classes cities
according to economic strength, number of inhabitants and
per capita income. There are a number of such lists with four
to six tiers. Everyone in China knows these rankings, and anyone wanting to do business, invest in real estate or relocate
studies them very carefully.

First-tier cities are usually only the megacities—Beijing,
Shanghai, Shenzhen and Guangzhou. As development is so

dynamic, the finance magazine *Yicai Global* introduced an extra category of "Top 15 New First-Tier Cities" in 2017 that included Chengdu, Hangzhou and Qingdao, among others. Of the subsequent 30 two-tier cities, many fall into the "never heard of them outside China" category. There are 70 third-tier, 90 fourth-tier and 129 fifth-tier cities.

I sip my fifth-tier coffee and comb through profiles on the Couchsurfing app, a truly laborious task, as it soon becomes apparent that many members haven't logged in for years and it is highly likely that they are not active anymore. Others, however, have such interesting profiles that I can't wait to meet them—for instance, the artist Lin in Beijing who tells me on WeChat that the police recently demolished her studio. She invites me to visit her and promises to tell me the rest of her story. Or a thirty-four-year-old man named Sung Kim who runs a restaurant in Dandong from which you can look across the river to North Korea. I'm very happy when he sends me an invitation to stay for two nights.

Then the film crew comes to pick me up.

"Hello, welcome!" shouts Nora, an exuberant bundle of energy, almost five feet tall, with alert dark eyes and a conspicuously high-pitched voice that sounds as if she wants to drown out anyone within a twenty-foot radius. Looking into the camera and speaking into a mic, she launches off: "This is Stephan, our guest from Germany!"

I say hello to my traveling companions for the next few days: couchsurfer Nora, as well as a cameraman and a female reporter. They take me to a car where I get to meet Nora's husband, an artist with a Beatles hairstyle, and then we head off to a restaurant.

"You are invited, of course—hotels, food, everything," she says. "You are going to be very famous soon!"

I know that sentence from somewhere. The good old going-to-be-famous-in-China promise. A couple of weeks previously, I discovered Nora's online profile, where she wrote of a TV series she was producing about traditional villages of the Tujia ethnic minority. On receiving my email, she immediately invited me to join the show. Filming was due to last three days, and we would be accompanied by a team from Hunan TV, a broadcasting station producing a documentary about Nora's work in the villages. So I would also be appearing on that. Hunan TV is the second-most-popular channel in the country, after CCTV-I, with 210 million viewers per day. *At last, my plans for hitting the big time are moving forward,* I thought to myself as I accepted the invitation.

A short while later, I was astonished to discover that Nora had posted my WeChat profile photo in her "moments" without asking me first. The image from the Pitu app showing me in traditional wear accidentally resembles clothing of the Tujia people. Beneath it she had written: "With this personal picture our foreign brother expresses his greatest respect of the Tujia peoples! Poor villages will get the attention of the world and become international places of interest! Are they soon to be civilized places for tourists? Witness how we become independent and prosperous! We hope that our live show *Getting Rich* will shock the world!"

What an ambitious young lady. Before it comes to that, my new showbiz friends take me to a tiny restaurant named Sun Family Shrimps at the Southern Gate. The walls are bare and the cold lighting reminds me of an operating room. The floor is dotted with the leftovers of previous meals, but every table except the one reserved for us is full. The reason why soon becomes clear, as highly motivated waitresses deck the table with oysters in garlic sauce, clams and a huge pot of delicious bright red chili shrimp—haute cuisine served on cheap plastic tablecloths, accompanied by Harbin beer in plastic cups. What might seem incongruous from a narrow-minded Western viewpoint seems perfectly reasonable to the Chinese. What is wrong with a restaurant putting all its effort into the food instead of hanging pretty pictures on the wall and tidying up nonstop? And what if, additionally, the prices are affordable? However, the reverse—that every grubby-looking restaurant serves fantastic food—is also a misconception, as is the idea that the Chinese generally don't value outward appearances. You need look no further than the gaudy designs on packaging of all kinds of products from wine to cigarettes to cell phones, or the almost religious adoration of some luxury brand names. Our compartmentalized Western way of thinking—the either/ or of our perceptions—is constantly challenged in a country like China.

After the feast we drive to the Zhongxin Business Hotel, where the lobby flaunts a polished stone floor, walls overlaid with exotic woods and a signboard with inflated room rates that are three times the actual price so that guests feel like they are getting an incredible bargain.

Beyond the lobby, the facilities have seen better days. I share a twin room with the cameraman, a reserved man in his mid-twenties with horn-rimmed glasses. When he isn't operating his camera he is usually busy with his cell phone.

The only things in the room that can safely be classified as post-1985 are the calling cards with revealing photos and telephone numbers for sex workers that somebody slipped beneath the door, as well as the items for sale on a plywood shelf: playing cards, Red Bull, canned herbal teas, Wahaha bottled water and Nabs Standard condoms. The room smells of stale cigarette smoke and cat piss.

Via WeChat, Nora asks me to meet her at the escalator because she wants to talk to me about something.

"Our two companions work for the state media," she says. "That's why I haven't mentioned couchsurfing. The government is not too fond of it because it allows travelers to see not only the good things but also the bad. Do you understand?"

"No problem. I won't mention it either."

"We will just say that I came across you via your blog."

"Okay." I don't have a blog.

"Tomorrow we are going to the villages. We have already prepared something for you there."

"Oh, what?"

"It will be more fun if it's a surprise. Good night!"

105

LET'S TAKE A little detour to the subject of the media. The Chinese love rankings—but probably not ones from Reporters Without Borders about freedom of the press. In 2018, China was ranked 176 out of 180, which was thirty places behind Russia and twenty places behind Turkey, two other notoriously restrictive countries. Chinese journalists and bloggers who don't strictly toe the party line are intimidated constantly and can only bypass the omnipresent censors with plenty of courage and subtle allusions.

The state authorities regularly send orders to editors about what they are to report on and how. The independent news website *China Digital Times*, which operates out of the United States, publishes such stipulations under the Orwellian title Directives From the Ministry of Truth and sheds light on the censors' obsession with detail. In December 2017, for example, the government demanded the media avoid reports about Christmas, to counteract the "Westernization" of culture that celebrates "kitsch western holidays" and does not fit in with local traditions. This order was probably tilting at windmills; getting rid of Santa Claus for good seems quite unrealistic given the opulent Christmas decorations to be found in the stores and shopping districts in any Chinese megacity.

Other instructions from the Ministry of Truth are considerably less amusing:

Don't report or comment on the matter of child abuse at RYB Kindergarten in Beijing.[3]

Delete an article about smog causing 257,000 deaths in thirty-one cities in 2013.[4]

Don't report on a nationwide truck drivers' strike.[5]

Play down correlations between the stock market and trade conflict with the USA.[6]

Do not make further use of the slogan "Made in China 2025" [because of the realization that China's overconfident presence abroad was poorly received].[7]

Do not hype North Korea's latest nuclear test.[8]

During the annual National People's Congress, do not report on delegates' personal wealth. Do not report negatively on property markets, foreign exchange, the stock market, smog or traffic congestion.[9]

Do not hype the story of Ping-Pong player Fan Zhendong's defeat at the semifinals of the German Open championship.[10]

And time and again, when there are major accidents or industrial scandals: *All media must use Xinhua News Agency copy as a guide.*[11]

With a staff of more than eight thousand and 170 foreign offices, Xinhua is the largest news agency in the world. Unlike Associated Press or Reuters, they report in two directions. A substantial investigative department sniffs out scandals about which initially only the government is informed. Sometimes, a few weeks later, there are reports to the public about how the state leaders are tackling the problem.

Of course, Xinhua never criticizes the government. Maintaining harmony and stability is the primary declared publishing goal; depicting an accurate reflection of reality is secondary. A couple of years ago in Beijing I listened to a lecture by Yan Wenbin, a Xinhua boss. As a grand master of Chinese smokescreen rhetoric, he presented a rational-sounding explanation for withholding facts from the public: "We don't describe problems in such detail because readers are not able to solve them anyway," he said.

The other major state "not-describers" of problems are the fifty channels of CCTV, the newspaper group *People's Daily* and, most recently, a radio and TV consortium called Voice of China, which is trying to gain a stronger standing internationally.

107

Most Chinese people get their information from the news-and-gossip cocktail served up online. WeChat is an immensely important source, as is the microblogging site Weibo. Between 2009 and 2012, something outrageous was going on, something that had been unthinkable in all of China's five-thousand-year history. For three years, an almost undisturbed exchange of information was possible. The censorship authorities were lagging behind and didn't monitor or control what was being posted on Weibo. Millions of users publicly discussed food scandals, environmental pollution and the government's mistakes. All of a sudden there was a civilian society that talked about problems openly, and for the first time, readers were aware of the true magnitude of some of these scandals.

Years of absorbing propaganda led to considerable dissatisfaction in the country, and the Communist Party came in for some hefty criticism. When in 2011 two bullet trains collided near Wenzhou, people first heard of the catastrophe on Weibo. Two years later Xi Jinping, who had at that time only been in power for one month, banned any online posts that "threatened" the reputation or interests of the party or national

108

security. On top of this, the Weibo profiles of known critics of the regime were deactivated. The short period of open debate that nobody had thought was possible was over. The nightmare of reality reverted to a state of blissful ignorance.

Xi Jinping has proven to be a hard-liner when it comes to the control of information. The list of forbidden terms in social and traditional media becomes ever longer.

During my travels, the news and entertainment app Toutiao attracted the attention of the authorities. With 120 million users a day, it was a huge success that offered not only popular videos and cartoons but also the option of sorting the kind of news the user was interested in. Theoretically, you could choose to read only about sports or celebrity gossip, or watch only videos of scantily clad ladies—and, for instance, block anything to do with the Communist Party. The state radio and TV regulators criticized the "vulgar content" and shuttered the affiliated jokes app Neihan Duanzi. The public letter of apology from the Toutiao CEO, Zhang Yiming, sounded as if he had written it with someone holding a gun to his head. He confessed to violating the core socialist values, disregarding Xi Jinping's guidelines and only making halfhearted attempts to shift opinion in a positive direction. But all these mistakes would be corrected in the future, he promised.

The government's strategy of keeping unpleasant facts and opinions out of the public eye has worked surprisingly well, considering there are 1.4 billion people here and a global internet where you can normally find information about every imaginable topic in seconds. But the Great Firewall blocks access to all major foreign news agencies, as well as Google, Facebook and Twitter, and access to VPN servers is made more and more difficult.

And apparently the Chinese people don't want to know everything. This was demonstrated by an experiment by researchers from Stanford and Peking Universities in which 1,800 students were given the chance of installing free VPN access for eighteen months. The scientists were interested in discovering how many would seize the opportunity to access foreign information and news sources: sites in Taiwan or Hong Kong, for instance, or the Chinese editions of the *New York Times* or *Financial Times*. They wondered whether it would be almost all of them? Half? A quarter? Their guesses weren't even close—the answer was a paltry 5 percent. Brainwashing is working so well in China that it seems the vast majority of people don't expect to find anything interesting outside the country.

Censorship Trivia

1 Images of Winnie-the-Pooh were banned on the Chinese internet after memes comparing Xi Jinping to Pooh became popular.

2 *Hexie* means "harmony," and "to harmonize" is a euphemism for "to censor." Because *hexie* can also mean "freshwater crab," regime critics use pictures of the animal when writing critically about censorship.

3 When the term "MeToo" was banned on Weibo, people started using *"mi tu"* (rice bunny) instead.

4 Many Weibo posts about Taylor Swift's album *1989* actually refer to a massacre—the year and the singer's initials allude to the Tiananmen Square protests.

> 5   The Chinese word for "dictator" sounds like the word for
> "poisonous vegetable" (both are *ducai*), so the character
> for the latter is often used to describe the former.

The students in the research study were then given a quiz with money as a reward. To get the correct answers, it was necessary to visit Western news sites, and suddenly things looked different. Now, ten times the number—so 50 percent—of students who had activated their VPN accounts were interested in the information on offer, and they spent a longer time on the sites. In the questionnaire afterwards, they admitted to being more critical of the Chinese government than before and less optimistic about the future of their country. And, at last, they were interested in continuing to read foreign news sources via VPN. But—and this is a big but—they had to be directed there. Open internet alone was not enough, for most of them, to make them want to discover information that had been withheld in their country. The study showed that censorship can work even if there are loopholes, the kind of censorship that is *chabuduo*, which means "good enough but not perfect." China was a *chabuduo* country for a long time, but President Xi is imagining a shift away from this. He wants total control of information and opinions.

HEARTS
AND THUMBS-UPS

O**N OUR WAY** through the villages, we cruise through what seem like antiquated surroundings in our silver Buick Excelle. Buffaloes pull plows through rice paddies; in roadside restaurants, bamboo steamers are filled with *baozi* (stuffed buns); and dogs and pigs wander around freely. Picturesque wooden farmhouses topped with dark gray tiled roofs stand next to functional two-story concrete buildings that seem to have come from a prefab catalogue. Very often, old and new completely fail to blend, as if there has been an anti-architecture competition, the winner being the new building that fits in least organically with the surroundings: explicitly permitted are purple walls, diagonal patterns with off-white tiles and barred windows for the prison look.

I woke up in a bad mood, and the view is not making it better.

"The villagers buy modern houses because they think it is what everyone is doing, so it must be good," says Nora. "The people are sadly not well educated, have little self-confidence and don't realize how valuable their traditions are. With our TV series we want to show them that even rich people would love a life like it is in a Tujia village—a rich foreigner like you, for instance."

So, okay, I'm about to be exploited again. But, just maybe, here it will serve a good purpose.

"Tell me if you need to go to the bathroom," she adds.

"Will do."

"Do you need to go to the bathroom?"

"No."

"You can take a nap now."

"No worries, I like looking out of the window."

"I hope you're not bored."

"I. Am. Not. Bored!"

"You sure?"

"Yes."

Chinese solicitude, however well meant, can sometimes really get on your nerves. Especially after being on the move for a couple of weeks, after a few nights with little sleep and on one of those travel days when my head feels bleary and new impressions are not proving to be a relief. Today, five lions could cross the road doing handstands and I would just think, *So what?* and be too lazy to get my camera out of my backpack. Overnight, it's as if I've become a different person, someone lethargic and complacent.

Whoever thinks that long-term traveling must feel like being drunk in a hammock for sixteen hours a day hasn't really tried it. The illusion that an interesting or even famous place is enough in itself to inspire that precisely predictable feeling of well-being disregards what a flighty thing one's own mood can be.

On top of that, I'm with TV people—I don't like being filmed. They won't even tell me what they have planned for me, and most of the time they are speaking Chinese, laughing a lot, and only occasionally do I catch single words, such as "straight ahead," or "Tujia" or "house." In a car with four cheerful Chinese people, for the first time on my travels here, I feel lonely. But I try to hide my bad mood from the others.

Nora's husband, a chipper guy in a beige jacket with a horse design on the back, nudges me regularly, pointing out the window and saying, "Beautiful."

"He only knows two or three English words," Nora tells me, and lays her arm over his shoulder.

In a place called Matouxi ("horse head river village") we stop in front of a new wooden house with curved rooftop and colorful displays of the Tujia culture in the courtyard. We have an appointment with the mayor, a small man who certainly doesn't look like a typical villager with his suit and patent-leather shoes, and who offers us expensive cigarettes but doesn't smoke himself when we decline.

The camera's on, and Nora does a short interview with him for Hunan TV. He says there are three hundred houses in Horse Head River Village and six hundred inhabitants. This year, no one here is living below the poverty line, but without new sources of money, the village will hardly be able to survive.

"Would more tourists be good?" Nora asks.

"Of course," he replies.

Looking in my direction, he adds: "Couldn't you do something about it?"

"We'll see," I say. Everybody wants something from me, and I just want to go back to bed and not have to talk to anyone, but nobody asks me what I want.

And then the folklore program begins.

First, we walk to a replica of an old rapeseed oil press. Three tanned men ram a tree trunk suspended from a roof rafter against a giant mortar. They swing it back and forth twice, and then ram with the third swing, accompanied by shouts of "Eeeja, eeeja, hu!" With every "Hu!"—which is very similar to the battle cry whooping of Icelandic soccer fans—some more drops of oil are extracted from the seeds in the mill.

"And now you," commands Nora. "Put this on and join in."

She gives me a plastic bag with pants and a sweater made of black silk—a traditional Tujia outfit embroidered in a colorful pattern of small flowers that bears an uncanny resemblance to my WeChat profile picture. Spectacularly overdressed, I join the tree-trunk rammers on the oil press.

"You have to chant louder; otherwise, people will think you're not working hard!" says Nora, who is filming this with her phone. I chant louder.

Afterwards, we travel on to our next stop at a bridge. Women in red outfits and men wearing something similar to my clothing are performing some songs. Some of them have scribbled the text on their hands, and the best singer is wearing a headdress full of jingling silver ornaments. I am supposed to join them by singing half a verse for television. For someone with an average talent for languages and a singing ability somewhere between that of a soccer fan and a kid in confirmation class, this is an impossible endeavor. An old, wrinkly Tujia woman repeats the melody five times, but I'm unable to imitate the dialect of the lyrics and unusual tone intervals. She looks at me like an elementary school teacher who sees a child sweating over the sum of three plus three.

Nora calls a crisis meeting. She suggests that I just join in for the final yell at the end of the song, a "*Jiaaa jiah!*" with a lunging step forward and everyone sticking out their right arms. After two takes, it's in the can. Even the mayor, who just arrived by car, is grinning happily. Then he organizes the obligatory group photos at the end of the bridge.

"You have your husband tonight, so you won't be lonely," he says to Nora. "Who has got the German?"

"Hmm. Maybe the dog?" Nora replies.

Everyone laughs. I am just a dog joke on this trip. From the perspective of today's grouchy mood, Horse Head River Village represents the dismal reality of what travel brochures try to promote as the "unspoiled charm of an authentic village with a cultural program typical of the region."

Screw being famous; I just want to go home and hide, away from people and cameras.

But that's not an option.

"We now have to look for a house that my husband can paint," declares Nora, once we are sitting in the car again. "You can take a break."

I look silently out the window at the ancient beauty of green fields and farmhouses in the afternoon mist.

"Stephan," Nora announces a few minutes later.

"Yes?"

"You're a writer, aren't you? Don't you want to write a poem?"

"A poem?"

"Yes."

"About what?"

"The trees, the flowers, the animals."

"No."

"Are you bored?"

"No!"

Eventually, we stop in front of a particularly decorative wooden house built on stilts on a slope. Two bird carvings decorate the uneven roof ridge, clucking chickens roam around and an old man in a suit and with a walking stick is selling honey.

Nora turns on her cell camera and asks him how important it is for him to keep his house.

"I will care for it until the day I die," he says.

"Why?"

"The first reason is that I don't have the money to build a new one. The second reason is everybody says that it is an important cultural asset. And we agree."

Nora's husband, the artist, looks for a spot outside and gets out his ink, paintbrushes and paper.

"With those paintings, we want to raise awareness of the beauty of these old buildings," Nora explains. He has already painted three thousand houses, and they have been exhibited in Beijing, Canada and Slovenia. "Actually, I gave him the idea. I think he does it mostly to please me." They have been a couple for five years and married for three.

"Beautiful," says the artist, as if he noticed we were talking about him. Then the Hunan TV guys interview him.

I go for a short walk and marvel at the huge water buffaloes the farmer is using to plow the rice field next to the neighboring house. Below, men are washing spring onions in the mud-colored river, and on the road a couple of yards above them is a propaganda poster declaring that the fight against poverty is the party's main objective.

As it is getting dark, we move on. Our accommodation is a simple homestay in a renovated wooden house that gets its electricity from a couple of solar panels.

"Tomorrow, we have more than an hour of live broadcast, so have a good rest," says Nora. "By the way, you can take off the Tujia clothes now."

I read a bit more online about the Tujia people, one of fifty-five ethnic minorities in the country. Eight million Chinese people belong to the group, and their culture is more than one thousand years old. One particular tradition is still upheld: during the last month before a wedding ceremony, the bride wails for one hour every day. Initially, she does this alone, but after a couple of days, her mother, grandmothers, aunts and sisters join in for communal lamentations. Even on the day of the wedding, a couple of heavy sobs are expected from the bride if she wants to be considered virtuous. Some mothers even send their teenage daughters to crying workshops; after all, everything can be learned.

Are the Tujia men really that bad? Or are the women just bemoaning the loss of innocence? Both wrong: the women believe that following a strict prescription of advance wailing will ensure the marriage will not be a joyless one. Additionally, they are mourning the bride leaving her family and, traditionally, also the failure of the marriage broker to find a better groom (nowadays, however, the role of marriage brokers in choosing partners is greatly reduced). The more tears the bride weeps, the more riches are in store for her family. Yet everything needs a counterbalance: at traditional burials the Tujia people sometimes dance half the night, as they don't think of death as a sad event.

. . . .

THE NEXT MORNING, a trip to the "Good Heart" rice wine distillery is on the schedule. The wine is 60 percent alcohol and made with a special mixture of seventy-seven herbs.

"You need a good heart to make healthy wine," the owner says in explanation of the name.

My experience of tasting it tells me that, rather, you need a strong heart to drink it.

Back in the courtyard of our accommodations we meet an old bamboo basket maker and a weaver.

"He will show you how he works, and then we will have a little competition," explains Nora. "Soon we will be live for half an hour on Yingke."

Yingke is a streaming app for live videos, similar to Periscope, with an additional function that enables viewers to transfer money directly to presenters they like.

"Ready?" asks Nora. She switches her smartphone to video mode, holds it in front of her with a selfie stick and greets the viewers. The Hunan TV crew film Nora filming us with her phone, and a surveillance camera in the courtyard films all of us.

"San, er, yi—three, two, one. Go!" shouts Nora, and the competition begins.

The old man and I both have half-finished bamboo baskets in front of us roughly the size of a beer barrel but much lighter. Dozens of strips of wood point upwards, and now another strip of pliable wood has to be woven through the upright pieces. Whoever finishes a complete circle first is the winner.

Nora commentates like a sports reporter in Chinese and English. She screams and fools around without remaining still for a second. On her screen hearts and thumbs-ups are appearing.

My weaving skills exhibit more enthusiasm than precision, which might have something to do with the rice wine. After almost a minute, I've completed nearly a quarter of the bamboo circle and am pretty proud of myself. I glance to my right—the pro, a little man with a weather-beaten face and plenty of laugh lines, has finished long ago. China versus Germany: 1–0. The pro helps me make my basket look something like a basket.

120

Nora asks me my opinion of village traditions. I stress how much I appreciate Chinese traditions, particularly as a foreign tourist, and tell her I wish people would appreciate the value of old cultural techniques more.

I have to use some self-control not to look at the screen the whole time because the program has an automatic beautifying function that gives us all large eyes and perfect skin. Heart, heart, thumbs-up.

We move on to a weaving chair, where an old lady shows me how to weave blankets with traditional patterns. Nora screams her comments; I notice that I'm getting a headache from the alcohol.

Half an hour goes by in a flash, and afterwards, Nora checks the statistics to see how many viewers we had: up to 34,000 at one point.

"Later the video will be shown on other channels, and then there will be considerably more viewers," Nora promises.

She makes another film with me, an interview for a news portal called Tiantian Kuaibao, which means "every day quick news." This time the interview is about me: my previous travels and my experiences in China until now. I talk about my books, my favorite countries—Iran, Greenland and Nepal—the casinos in Macau, the cats in Shenzhen and the unconventional meal in Wenshi. I don't mention couchsurfing.

"Are you going to write a book about China?" asks Nora.

"No," I reply.

Nora says good-bye to the viewers and looks somewhat puzzled at the statistics. "Strange—only six viewers. There's something wrong, usually it's at least eighty thousand." She calls the editor responsible for the program and they talk briefly. Nora seems troubled.

"There's a new law since the beginning of this month," she says after ending the call. "Interviews with foreigners can no longer be broadcast live, only after a time lag of ten days. The material has to be checked."

"Did we say something controversial?"

"You said something about eating dogs. That's a tricky subject."

"Why?"

"In a number of Chinese regions it is normal. The people there shouldn't feel they are doing something wrong. Maybe the editors will cut it."

"Have you ever had problems with censorship?"

"Once an African-American talked a lot about politics and criticized Trump. That wasn't allowed on our show. We don't want to fuel the conflict between America and China. We have to be careful."

On my cell I discover a new friendship request. "Hello, my name is Nature. I saw the live interview with you," a woman writes. "Nice to meet you!"

Her profile photo shows a palm pointing towards the camera. It is difficult to say whether it is a friendly gesture or a defensive one. Her right eye is hidden by her fingers, and her left eye looks intently at the viewer, so intently that you could get nightmares from it. As she was one of six viewers, she must work for the censorship department of the broadcaster. I decide to delete her request.

From: Yang Berlin
Hey, how's it going? You famous yet?

To: Yang Berlin
I was on an internet TV show!

From: Yang Berlin
A dating show?

To: Yang Berlin
No, about the traditions of the Tujia

From: Yang Berlin
Oh, I see. Boring

· · · · · · · · · ·

AS FAR AS schools go, I thought I had developed a certain routine. Until my appearance, that is, at the high school in Yuanguping, a village consisting of some 40 percent houses and 60 percent building sites for more houses. We meet roughly a hundred schoolkids, all between twelve and fourteen years old, on a basketball court in the schoolyard. Nora and the Hunan TV crew accompany me to the middle of the court. After the teacher greets me in English and introduces me to the kids, my trials begin. I feel a bit like the kung fu novice in The 36th Chamber of Shaolin.

The first trial: Shake hands with one hundred schoolkids. They introduce themselves in English, and I answer, "Hello, my name is Stephan," and we both say: "Nice to meet you."

One hundred hands is an awful lot.

The second trial: Sing a song. The kids gather around in a circle and I get a headset mic and a loudspeaker to hang around my neck, which looks like a very old Walkman portable music player and distorts my voice badly.

"Could you sing a song for us?" asks the teacher.

"Unfortunately, I can't sing," I reply.

"Then sing something with the kids!" She calls two girls to the front who proceed to sing a Chinese song to the tune of

123

"Twinkle, Twinkle, Little Star." Because I don't know the words, I just hum along a bit.

The third trial: Learn *da lian xiao*. This is a dance with a bamboo stick with red and yellow pom-poms attached to each end. A boy shows me how to hit the knee and foot with the stick in rhythm; the result reminds me of Bavarian folk dances. The kids applaud.

The fourth trial: Act like a sergeant major. The kids form a number of lines in front of me, and then I'm supposed to say, "Up," "Down," "Left," or "Right," and they have to crouch, jump up, and turn ninety degrees left or right as quickly as possible. The ones who make a mistake are out. They react pretty promptly but are not always right, and at the end there is only one boy remaining. He is then granted a wish.

The fifth trial: Grant the boy's wish that I play basketball. A hundred kids gather around me to watch five free throws. Twice I miss, twice I hit the rim and once I make a basket: massive applause.

"Now that they like you, we can begin the classes," says Nora.

We relocate to room 194 in the three-story school building. "Be honest and work hard" is written in large red characters on the back wall. I introduce myself, speak a bit about my job and explain why I like the English language so much. Then comes the round of questions: "How old are you?" "What is your favorite animal?" "Do you like Chinese food?" "Do you like large and small worms crawling all over you?" Uh-oh, I wasn't prepared for that one, but the answer isn't too difficult.

Then the teacher asks them to write me a letter in English or Chinese, and while they do this I go to the neighboring classroom and go through my program once more.

124

On leaving, I get almost a hundred letters, as well as presents: paper airplanes, paper birds, origami hearts; a Plasticine figure with blue eyes and yellow hair; a pencil with a dragon's head eraser; a cuddly toy monkey and a stuffed dog. *In China, you can be whatever you want*—Yang's words reappear in my mind. I am truly overwhelmed and declare that my mission to be famous has been accomplished. I'm like a celebrity for those kids. It won't get any better than this.

· · · · · · · · · ·

ON THE DRIVE back to the city Nora tells me something about her strong connection to the villages. She now speaks unusually quietly, almost whispering, because she has caught a cold and is a bit hoarse.

"When I was five, my family's old wooden house was demolished for a road building project. We didn't get any compensation." The artist holds her hand; he can feel that she is upset, even though he doesn't know what she is saying. "Today I am fighting to preserve these cultural assets. The Chinese must finally learn that 'old' does not necessarily mean 'poor.' Old can also mean great richness."

I suddenly realize the great injustice I had done Nora when I was in a bad mood at the beginning of our trip. In truth, her harmless, entertaining online TV format is the most intelligent way of reaching as many people as possible. If she were to report on the cultural uniqueness of the Tujia people in the tone of an ethnologist, she would only reach a fraction of viewers. If she were to condemn in a sharper tone the modernization as a scandal, she wouldn't be able to broadcast much longer. By featuring a foreigner on her show, on the one hand, she is telling the villagers how interesting their culture is for

125

travelers from all corners of the world, and on the other, she is making the program a bit funnier and more unusual for the public. Nora is a genius, and I'm an idiot because I only realized it on the return journey.

"How do you finance the program?" I ask her.

"I work as an English teacher and translator. I've also won a couple of competitions. With my degree in journalism from the USA I could start a very successful career elsewhere. But I think I've found my purpose here."

"Beautiful," says her husband, pointing at an old wooden house and a rice paddy in the mist.

DANDONG

Population: 2.4 million

Province: Liaoning

THE RESTAURANT
AT THE END OF
THE WORLD

NORA AND HER companion drop me off at Zhangjiajie Hehua International Airport. My journey continues now to Dandong in the northeast. My host, Sung, lives twenty miles farther north but is busy tonight, which is why I will spend my first night in the middle of the city. Not the worst option, as the Zhonglian hotel offers one of the most interesting views in all of China, so interesting, in fact, that high-performance binoculars come with every room. "For your convenience of exotic scenery," says a note, along with the information that there will be a five-hundred-yuan (seventy-U.S.-dollar) fine in the event of loss.

From the eighth floor, the first view is of a busy street with two lanes in one direction and three in the other. To the right stands a sand-colored high-rise with a massive billboard advertising a real estate project called Seventh Mansion. Beyond the road flows the Yalu, meaning "green duck," as the curving course of the river is thought to resemble a duck's neck. A pleasure boat is docked at a pier, and to the left, one and a half bridges stretch towards the other bank.

The half bridge just goes to the middle of the river since it was destroyed by U.S. Air Force bombs in 1950. Today, the remains are a tourist attraction with red Chinese flags fluttering from all the stays of the truss bridge.

The complete bridge, the Friendship Bridge, links to Sinuiju in North Korea. It is the most important land connection for trade between the two countries. When North Korea's dictator, Kim Jong-un, traveled to Beijing for a state visit in March 2018, his train crossed the border here behind specially erected screens. It is only 100 miles from Dandong to Pyongyang and a good 250 miles to Punggye-ri, the nuclear test site that was in operation until 2018.

I pick up the binoculars and take a look at the opposite bank. I can see two cranes and a couple of high-rises that are of conspicuously plainer construction than their Chinese counterparts. I can also see the white framework of a roller coaster and a Ferris wheel, both of which look as if they haven't been used for a long while.

A border of more than 620 miles links China and North Korea: two different worlds but with only a couple hundred yards of water between them, here the Yalu and farther north the Tumen. This proximity is one of the reasons for the close cooperation between the two regimes. If there was a coup in North Korea, a refugee crisis would be unavoidable. In the Korean War of the early 1950s, China supported their Communist brothers in the north. However, since Pyongyang carried out the first nuclear test in October 2006, the relationship has taken a knock. Beijing is not too thrilled about having a nuclear-armed neighbor. Nevertheless, China is by far North Korea's most important economic partner, accounting for 90 percent of their foreign trade.

· · · · · · · · · ·

A CAB WITH cute stuffed dogs on the dashboard takes me north the next day, always following the course of the border river. The bleak fields on the far bank are various pastel shades of brown and yellow. On the Chinese side, however, there are modern apartment blocks, patriotic sculptures with red scarves and warning signs with cartoonlike illustrations that proclaim: "Appreciate the good life! Abide by the border regulations!" Here, the threat of a prison sentence is disguised as a calendar motto.

I ask the young driver whether he would rather live here or on the other side of the river, expecting a patriotic affirmation of China. Instead, he answers philosophically: "Every life has joys and suffering. If I were born over there, I would probably also find reasons to be happy."

Human-sized soapstone sculptures of the twelve signs of the zodiac mark my objective: the Korean restaurant of Sung and his family.

129

Sung greets me with a North Korean "Dragon and Phoenix" cigarette drooping from the corner of his mouth. "These are better than the Chinese: very strong and only eighty-five yuan [twelve U.S. dollars] per pack," he says.

He is thirty-six years old, a little over six feet tall, with thick bangs, chubby cheeks and the fashionable Adidas chic of a Korean pop star. At the same time, however, he seems sensitive and almost aristocratic, like a lord of the manor receiving me in his realm. We cross the front garden, in which there is a statue of *harubang*, a Korean fertility god, and enter a dining room with a fine view of the river and the neighboring country. Sung originally comes from South Korea and, with his passport, has no chance of entering North Korea. Every day, he looks out of his window at a no-go zone, only 430 yards away but unreachable.

In the background water splutters in an aquarium where three fish are spending their last hours. Opposite the window are tall glass cylinders with pickled ginseng roots inside.

"When my father came here twenty years ago, he was mostly dealing in ginseng," says Sung. "The more the shape of the root resembles the human anatomy, the stronger its healing properties are supposed to be." He tells me that some ginseng products can apparently make gray hair black again.

He then points out a container filled with a reddish rice wine and a dead snake. It seems to be looking out the window towards North Korea. "Six feet long. We found it here in the garden," he explains. "We put it into the alcohol while it was alive; otherwise, its effects become weaker." Such a drink is supposed to fortify and increase potency. Kim Jong-un is believed to have experimented with snake wine to help him with his wishes for a second son. Now he is thought to have three children, but nobody knows for sure.

Sung offers to drive me to the little riverside harbor, and soon we are sitting in his parents' decrepit station wagon and listening to North Korean music on the radio: pompous violins, sentimental melodies and patriotic lyrics accompanied by static. To the left of the road we spot a brand-new fortress-like entrance with a ticket office leading to the easternmost remains of the Great Wall. This is the only part of the gigantic structure still located at a state border today. There isn't a single tourist on the site, though there is room for thousands.

Sung translates one of the songs on the radio: "At the moment it is about how much the singer misses Kim Jong-un's grandfather. She hopes to see him in a dream," he explains. The next song is about the hardship of a soldier's life, which can only be tolerated because the "supreme leader" is keeping an eye on his loyal troops.

We reach a jetty with white pleasure crafts with Chinese flags fluttering at their sterns. Sung says good-bye, as he has to work in the restaurant. I buy a ticket and go straight to the upper deck, where I mingle with quite a number of baseball-capped, outdoor-jacketed fellow travelers, with 600 mm zoom lenses on their cameras. They look like they're on safari.

131

A vendor offers grilled shrimp on a skewer. A loudspeaker announcement from the captain emphasizes that photos of small fishing boats and soldiers are forbidden, and anyone who disobeys the rule is personally responsible for the consequences.

As the boat sets off on the Green Duck River, the oncoming wind smells of brackish water and industrial dust. The boat is tilted slightly, as all the passengers on the deck are standing on the port side.

There, two farmers roughly five hundred yards away are working a field with pickaxes. Dozens of shutters click, some of them audibly on continuous shooting mode, taking eight or twelve photos per second.

Then we see two oxcarts at the riverbank, with the driver, dressed in rags, gathering seaweed. The scene, like a historical reenactment in an open-air museum, is photographed extensively. It's hard to imagine, but just twenty-five years ago, the per capita income in North Korea was higher than in China. For some of the older tourists, this trip must seem like a journey into their own past.

From the deck, one of the Chinese passengers waves and whistles, trying to attract attention. No reaction; the socialist brothers don't wave back. Until recently, the tour operators sold packages with bread and cookies to throw overboard but this has stopped.

Maybe you don't have to travel all the way to the border with North Korea to discover how absurd tourism can be, but this excursion of dictatorship voyeurs paying nine dollars for a ninety-minute trip is a prime example. We get to see a crumbling military fortress, a man riding a motorbike on a dirt track, two rowboats, two solar panels, three light green watchtowers, a couple of other people working in the fields and three soldiers on their way back to the barracks. What on earth do they think of the ships that do their rounds here every day? Are they told that people are curious because North Korea is the model socialist state, an example to others? Or do they feel like they're part of a folklore program in a human zoo as soon as they make an appearance on the riverbank? And what goes through their heads when they see that the roads and buildings on the other side of the river are in much better condition?

Nobody reacts to the repeated whistles of the man so keen to make contact. I find his behavior outrageous, but I have to ask myself why I find this photo safari so fascinating, even though there is nothing spectacular to see and it feels very wrong to be gaping at poor people from a safe distance, without making contact, without meeting them face-to-face. The answer is probably because the experience is so exclusive, because I have read enough about Kim Jong-un's unusual country that even the sight of the dullest of riverbanks has an aura of something special. But maybe it's also because I'm surprised by the archaic simplicity. From all I know about the egos of autocratic leaders, I would have expected more effort to show off a positive picture of the hermit kingdom.

. . . .

"I ONCE HAD a guest from France who was desperate to sleep with a North Korean because he knew that it would impress people back home," Sung tells me two hours later, when I meet him at the restaurant. "He didn't succeed, as they are all pretty well sealed off here."

A couple of thousand North Koreans work in Dandong: in restaurants where they serve and present karaoke shows, or

133

in the textile or electronics industries. The usual wage is three thousand yuan (US$425) a month, with half of it going to the North Korean state. They reside in isolated living quarters and are under constant surveillance. People who try to escape can get their families at home into serious trouble, as they are liable for the workers. North Korean refugees caught in China are repatriated and face prison sentences and torture.

Nevertheless, people still try to reach southwest China without using public transport, on foot, with human smugglers or by hitchhiking. One common route is via Myanmar to Thailand and from there to South Korea, where they have a chance of being recognized as refugees.

"And some Chinese men buy North Korean wives," Sung tells me, while turning on an electric grill on a round table and draping pieces of pork belly over it. "They have no passports and no rights. They're totally dependent on their husbands."

He opens a bottle of Yalu River beer and pours two glasses. "I don't like refugees," he says suddenly. "Everything they say is a lie. Well, that applies to at least ninety-nine percent of them. How many of them actually have problems for political reasons? Most of them just have something to hide. Maybe they have committed a crime. There might even be murderers among them."

"Aren't there thousands of reasons for wanting to leave North Korea? Starvation. Oppression. Lack of freedom?" I ask.

"If you don't like the system, you have to work from the inside to change it, not simply run away." He lights up a North Korean cigarette.

"That's easy to say. In Western countries people can demonstrate, or change things at the next election. In dictatorships things don't work like that."

"Yeah, and then they elect someone like the current American president. There, too, people's opinions are manipulated. I think things are much better in North Korea than they were ten years ago. Less famine, and the economy is picking up."

"Look out of the window. The way they are farming—it's like the beginning of the last century."

"They don't see anything of the outside world, so they have nothing to compare to. I think the North Koreans are happy."

This is a remarkable statement from someone who has lived in a pretty house with a view of the border river for six years. Every morning at seven he hears the distorted loudspeaker propaganda announcements extolling the "supreme leader," and in the afternoons he sees people washing their clothes in the gray-brown waters.

Sung himself has seen quite a bit of the aforementioned "outside world." During his philosophy studies, he lived in the Philippines. He worked in Australia for a year and went on a European tour with a church choir to Germany, Italy and France. A year ago he married a Chinese woman who lives around forty miles farther north. They see each other on the weekends. Sung is here to stay, and he has great plans for a twenty-seven-room hotel next door with a view of North Korea—the foundation is already in place.

"We want to open in two or three years, but there's still lots to do. And plenty of bureaucracy," he says, refilling the beer glasses. The pork belly is as tender as can be, sizzling and filling the room with its mouth-watering smell. There are side dishes of kimchi, bean sprouts and pickled cucumbers.

For his hotel, Sung needs a commercial license, approvals from the health and hygiene authorities, a fire protection permit and tax registration. Additionally, he must comply with various environmental requirements, be considered harmless by the secret services and, every now and then, allow functionaries to feast there for free.

"Compared to opening a hotel in China, my three years of military service was a piece of cake! Do you feel like a footbath?"

A short while later we are sitting in his room with our pant legs rolled up and our feet in plastic buckets filled with hot water, and I ask him whether he is happy. He considers this a while.

"For me, happiness is my family, being with my parents, with my wife. We want to have a child soon. People have different amounts of money, but everyone has a similar amount of time. I decided to spend most of mine with my family. Can't be beat. That's why it really doesn't matter what I'm doing in five or ten years—I know that I will be happy."

· · · · · · · · ·

THE NEXT MORNING, Sung and I are sitting together again in the restaurant and talking about Kim Jong-un's remarkable career. For years, he has been isolated as the outsider of global politics. Xi Jinping refused to meet with him, and obviously, Barack Obama and other Western leaders did too. But in 2018, he shook hands with Donald Trump in Singapore and had three meetings with Xi in Beijing and two with South Korea's head of state, Moon Jae-in.

"The situation is in flux. China would not be happy with a North Korean shift towards the USA," says Sung. "Even though both superpowers are in favor of nuclear disarmament. Kim Jong-un, in turn, knows that ending nuclear testing could endanger his power."

136

"What are the chances of a reunification of north and south?" I ask.

"There are a number of problems, in particular the enormous difference in economic strength. One country looks down on the other, even more so than was the case with the reunification of Germany."

"But would South Korea want reunification?"

"If it were to happen now, South Korea would have to spend an incredible amount of money for it. But if the North Korean economy were to improve, then it's conceivable. We were not separated by our own free will seventy years ago."

From one of the panoramic windows I observe a man on the far bank gathering water in a wooden bucket. Do you ever see people there having riverside picnics? Couples having a secret cuddle? Teenagers drinking beer and playing guitars? Almost certainly not. These thoughts distract me for a few moments, while Sung continues talking.

"I think Kim Jong-un wouldn't be against reunification. North Korea has the natural resources, the south the modern technology. Together, the country would have a population of 80 million, and it could be a great economic power, comparable to Japan."

"And at long last, you would be able to take a boat and row the forty yards from your house to the other side," I say.

"Yeah, crazy, isn't it?"

From: Lin Beijing
You can sleep in my studio. There are lots of paintings and sculptures there, I hope it won't bother you

To: Lin Beijing
No problem, sounds good!

From: Lin Beijing
I'm curious about what you think of China, this modern nazi dictatorship

PINKLAND

IN PINKLAND, THE trees and flowers are pink; the water, the stones and even the snow are pink, as are the houses, roads, cars, tanks, food, medicine and the walls that separate the country from the rest of the world. In Pinkland, there are no marriages, no class distinctions, no prisons—just love and liberty. If someone causes other people pain or harm, they will be immediately expelled. Citizenship, including a passport, is only granted to women and gay men. Straight men will be issued with visas for a maximum stay of ninety days. Decisions about permanent residency are made during a personal interview at which the applicant must wear pink clothing. The color pink stands for adjectives like sexy, pure, feminine, romantic, soft, relaxed and erotic, among others. Citizens reject bad colors such as black, blue and green; dye their hair pink; and wear pink-tinted contact lenses. Pinkland is a dictatorship, the currency is the pink crown and the emblem is two necking flamingos.

(Source: Pinkland information brochure)

THE CAB RIDE from the southern train station to where Lin lives on the eastern fringes of the city takes more than an hour, even in ideal traffic conditions. Beijing is huge, even by Chinese standards: a megacity with 6 million cars, 391 subway stations and more than seventy universities. Sluggish streams of vehicles edge along the highways, polluting the air; on the sidewalks, pedestrians with breathing masks hasten to their next appointments.

Since I've been traveling for a couple of weeks now, I should no longer feel a surge of awe and excitement at the sight of a cluster of high-rise buildings. But during this drive, I see so many newly built districts, and newly being built districts, that I wonder whether this reinforced concrete madness will ever end. Or will China just keep on building until there are no high-rise-free square miles in the whole country? Also striking are the giant propaganda billboards at the roadside; there are considerably more than on my last visit four years ago. In terms of self-promotion, Xi Jinping is as keen as Mao once was.

"Socialism with Chinese Qualities to Gain New Victories," "Realize the Great Dream" and "Great Struggles for a Great Project"—the slogans are presented in large yellow lettering against a red background. China is not hiding that it's heading for the top and aims to have a leading global role in the military, technological and economic sectors by 2049. From the Chinese viewpoint, Western dominance is merely a roughly 250-year interlude in history; after all, pre-1800, China had already been a world power for many centuries.

To realize this "great dream," there has been worldwide investment. The One Belt, One Road initiative—the new Silk Road—attracts trading partners with heavy credit for gigantic infrastructure projects. When Portugal was wallowing in its financial crisis of 2010–14, China was busy buying up companies and took over the port of Piraeus in Greece. And in Africa, China has long been the most important trading partner and is involved in more than one-third of all infrastructure projects. The Chinese assurance of not becoming involved in domestic affairs, unlike Western development aid organizations, has been very successful. And Xi likes to stress the similarity of being badly treated by the West: "We have shared similar experiences in the past. That's why there is such a close link between China and Africa," he said at a gathering of African heads of state. Despite some setbacks and much criticism, Xi has already achieved something there that most people thought impossible—most Africans believe that partnership with China does more for their economies than partnership with Western countries (in this context, it wasn't particularly bright of the current U.S. president to refer to some places in Africa as "shithole countries"; it is unthinkable that Xi would utter such a remark).

Whereas the West mostly considers Africa to be a crisis zone, China sees it as a place where an ever-growing middle class with purchasing power is developing: an excellent sales market for Chinese products, even high-tech toys or cars, so these are sectors that will expand in the coming years. And why shouldn't a number of countries be interested in the world's best surveillance systems or social credit software?

In the West, there is still little awareness of the speed with which this global economic power is advancing—or of the extent of its worldwide economic ties. The U.S. government overestimated how damaging a trade war would be for China. For sure it is hurting the economy, but it's far from being an existential threat. Xi Jinping can rely on the patriotism of his people to make it through some years with smaller economic growth.

· · · · · · · · ·

LIN IS WAITING for me on the main street. "It's a bit untidy at my place. I hope that's okay with you," she says.

We pass a barrier to her residential area, which consists of eight-story apartment blocks. She has hair almost to her hips and melancholic dark eyes. In her light blue rubber sandals, red leggings and brightly colored dress beneath a far-too-large woolen sweater, she looks like a fairy queen from a second-hand store. Sometimes when she's walking ahead of me, she sticks her arms out with her hands at right angles to her forearms, as if she were about to start flying.

Lin opens the door to the apartment and turns on the light, and all of a sudden we are surrounded by strange characters. Ahead of me, a sullen, grim-looking Kim Jong-un sits in a single-seater plane, releasing atomic rockets by pressing a button. Next to him, Xi Jinping and his wife wave from a group of cheerful teenagers. A child in a kimono rides a white swan, Mickey Mouse and Donald Duck pose on the Great Wall dressed in workers uniforms and a blonde girl with a pink octopus in her hair cleans her nails with a bread knife. On the floor lies a decapitated Venus de Milo painted pink, among countless tubes of paint, palettes and brushes.

Lin's pictures sit on easels or lean against the wall, one propped next to the other. There is not even close to enough space in the three-room apartment for an adequate gallery; there are even pictures leaning against the kitchen cupboards. Black-and-white plastic sheeting makes the floor look like an oversized chessboard. Being an artist in China is similar to playing a game of chess but less fun: tactical maneuvering and thinking ahead are important, because you often have to adapt to new situations and always live in fear of being checkmated.

"I had a huge studio on a five-thousand-square-mile piece of land in Songzhuang, half an hour from here. The state mafia destroyed it," she says, while waiting for the water to boil for tea. "They said something about an order to destroy seventy illegal buildings. I had rented the land for twenty years. When I began building there, they said it wasn't a problem. Two years later, they suddenly changed the law. That happens often with this nazi regime."

"Did they give you any warning?"

"They gave me a week to leave the house, but they came with two large bulldozers after three days. They destroyed thirty or forty artworks and one year of work getting things set up."

In Beijing, such incidences are common. Tens of thousands of residents were driven out of their homes in recent years, often under the pretext of dilapidated buildings having to be demolished for safety reasons. The people affected are mostly the poor—the new arrivals and migrant workers employed on

143

construction sites and in restaurants in the city. Beijing intends to destroy a total of ten thousand acres of "illegal" buildings and reduce the inner-city population by 2 million.

Very often it is artists who are victims of these measures. Many galleries have been destroyed, not only in Songzhuang but also in the Caochangdi art district, made famous by Ai Weiwei.

Lin is not sure whether her studio was targeted because she transformed it into an art project—Pinkland: a utopian dream world where everything revolves around the color pink, subtly criticizing a state where everything revolves around the color red.

"Artists are not welcome here. The government hates us," she says. Lin documented the demolition with photos and videos; she went to court a number of times, but her case was always rejected. She will certainly not be getting any compensation.

I ask her about her painting of Xi, the president and his wife waving happily, surrounded by smiling children—something about it seems off.

"Well spotted. I posted it on Weibo and got lots of likes because it seems so positive and patriotic." The story behind it, however, is different. "It is an exact re-creation of a propaganda photo of the Romanian dictator Ceaușescu. I just gave the children a more Chinese look and inserted our president. But, of course, the viewer doesn't know that."

Then she takes me to Pinkland, or what is left of it. One room in the apartment is full of relics: two Christmas trees, a radio set, a Venetian carnival mask, a wig, a sculpture of a female torso, baby dolls, a rubber chicken, towels and articles of clothing—everything in pink, even the walls.

Lin shows me deceptively real-looking Pinkland passports with flamingo motifs, pink crown banknotes and an information brochure with rules for citizens and visa applicants.

"I can even put a Pinkland stamp in your passport," she offers cheerfully.

At the moment, Lin is working on a film script about a fantasy world whose dictator forces people to feel free and happy. A dreamland enclosed behind a wall, where it is illegal to like any colors other than pink, where free love is practiced and where pink happiness pills are prescribed to cure sadness. A utopia somewhere between Barbie's *Dreamtopia* and Orwell's 1984, but lesbian. If I owned a film production company, I would immediately invest a heap of money in her project.

The studio apartment belongs to me for the night. Lin says good-bye and will sleep at her mother's home two hundred yards away. Her parents are divorced, but her father gave them three pieces of real estate.

The bedroom could have come straight out of a naughtier version of Tim Burton's *Alice in Wonderland*. The pink headboard, which has two handbags dangling from it, is decorated with two golden branches and between them in large letters is written "Lick Me, Baby." The decorations on the wall include a picture of Jesus with lambs and what looks like a medieval oil painting of an aristocratic lady with a painted-on mustache. The door, with "Queen Lin's Bedroom" written on it next to a painted crown, is guarded by a stuffed deer. Only the humming electronic air filter doesn't really fit in with this surreal collection.

145

When I go to brush my teeth in a dark green bathroom full of indoor plants, a grinning skull observes me from the windowsill. On the ground, there is a bust of Ludwig van

Beethoven and a rubber mask with the face of Hillary Clinton. This host certainly wins the award for the most original interior decoration of all the apartments that I have ever visited.

To: Nora Zhangjiajie
Hi Nora, has our interview been broadcast yet?

From: Nora Zhangjiajie
No, it's still being checked.

From: Nora Zhangjiajie
Maybe they will never broadcast it

Lin's WeChat profile photo shows Adolf Hitler in a pink uniform, and she is regularly posting things on Weibo that are deleted within minutes, or seconds, by diligent censors. When she wrote, "Long live the Dalai Lama," the police were at her front door within two hours. Her accounts have been blocked numerous times—ten thousand followers suddenly gone from one second to the next. But she doesn't give up, getting her information from banned foreign news portals and publishing her views on what is happening in the world. She is not afraid of serious consequences.

"They are looking for the big fish, not the little shrimp," she says.

IN NUMEROUS ARTICLES about artists and dissidents, you can read about what happens when people say things in China that don't toe the party line. Or you can spend half an hour in Lin's mother's living room.

The setting is unconventional. Between the sofa and the open-plan kitchen are the following decorations: a life-sized human skeleton for anatomy classes with a green hat on its skull; a picture on the wall of a child wearing a bloody eye patch and holding a fork, his own eye on a plate in front of him; a garden gnome; a display cabinet full of dolls; a porcelain flamingo; and much more.

In these surroundings, I witness an argument with her mother that Lin assures me is no exception but rather part of a long-running series of clashes; they fight on an almost daily basis. Lin talks in quiet, soft tones, unlike her mother, whose voice is loud and cutting, and who proceeds to clean up the kitchen with more noise than necessary. She appears wiry and fit enough to be ten rather than twenty years older than her daughter. As a yoga teacher and a vegetarian, she, too, is a nonconformist who lives her life differently from the generation before hers. Now and again, Lin translates and comments on her opponent's words, instead of answering immediately, which just makes the situation even more absurd.

Annotated Rantings
of a Patriotic Chinese Mother:

"Don't say anything bad about our country to him. Foreigners think our system isn't good, though every year things are improving. If you say too many negative things, then you should feel guilty about being Chinese because you hate this country."

I don't hate this country. She is acting as if party and country are the same, as if criticism of one is automatically criticism of the other. But they are two different things. I've tried so often to explain that to her.

. . . .

"You have no respect. You have to honor the party as you should honor your own parents and accept that they are always right. People who speak badly about their mothers are bad people."

I believe the government should be a service organization, not just like parents.

. . . .

"You're always complaining. Life is beautiful—you have enough to eat, enough fruit, you can live a healthy life. What more do you need? Why are you never satisfied?"

I don't know how to answer to this. But I simply feel that this government shouldn't turn the screws too tight. I told her I'm not complaining, it's just my opinion, I'm just saying what I think. If things are not going well, you should be able to criticize the government. Living a healthy life, for instance, is not so easy because nature is so polluted.

148

. . . .

"We can't do anything about the destruction of the environment. You don't have to drink water from rivers; you can get perfectly clean drinking water from stores. You don't think our country will die, do you?"

I just know that quite a lot is heading in the wrong direction. My mother doesn't feel this. I often think of leaving them. Mother and country. The decision is difficult for me. If I go, she will say I'm a bad person for leaving her behind.

. . . .

"You just make that rubbish and are wasting your life. Why can't you work as a teacher again, get married and have children? You are thirty-two. But stubborn as you are, I'm not surprised you can't find anyone."

The Chinese like subservient women. Sometimes I think that I'm strange or crazy and it's not surprising that nobody likes me. But when I was in Europe, people often spoke to me and men wanted my WhatsApp contact details. When I told my mother that, she refused to believe me.

. . . .

"And you forgot to do the washing up."

Oh, I think she's right.

They quarrel passionately, unforgivingly, neither budging from her position in this doll's-house-cum-ghost-train room that Lin designed. Interestingly, Lin's mother let her daughter decorate the living room even though she describes her art as "rubbish." In China, sometimes you have to look for evidence of parental love in deeds, not words.

Lin suggests that we take a look at Beijing's art scene. She orders a cab with her pink cell phone.

"I'm not really that strong. Actually, I'm small and weak," says Lin, still battered by the fight. "I only want to be myself,

149

but that seems to be not allowed." During the cab ride towards the city center via the Beijing–Harbin Expressway, she tells me of her lifelong struggle.

Lin started taking painting classes at ten, but even then, at school, just copying from other works bored her. She hated learning by obeying—independent thinking was not encouraged. Once, her art teacher shouted at her and wanted to throw her picture out the window because the colors she used were too bright—too much pink, even then. Schoolkids were drilled to think of individuality and freedom as unimportant. Instead, they were taught to serve their country, follow the party lines and be prepared to make sacrifices.

In music classes they sang patriotic songs. Lin remembers the lyrics of one of them: "Our motherland is like a garden, the flowers in the garden full of color. Our heads are like sunflowers, and there's always a smile on our faces." Lin felt that she was the only one in the classroom who was immune to the numbing magic of the sickly sweet melodies and lyrics. There was something wrong. Where were they, these gardens and flowers, and why didn't she feel like smiling all the time?

Lin's parents were so poor in the 1980s that she didn't have a single doll to play with, which is why she began collecting dolls as an adult. At home, she painted cartoon characters on her bedroom walls and was beaten as a punishment. She was never allowed to shut her door, and when she took a shower, her mother was often in the bathroom to talk to her. Always control, and no secrets, at any cost. Dictatorship at home, dictatorship at school.

After high school, Lin was accepted to a prestigious art college in Beijing, but even there new ideas were rare, little craziness was tolerated and no experiments were allowed. She revered the graffiti artist Banksy but had to emulate the Russian old masters. The most creative people in the city spent their student years copying traditional paintings. The meaning of art was defined by tutors, and discussing taboo topics or breaking the rules was unwelcome.

Lin still managed to pull through, because she didn't find the assignments particularly difficult. Once, she posted a photo of a university celebration with students on campus waving red flags next to a similar photo of a Nazi procession. Both photos were swiftly deleted.

She found a job teaching in a middle school, but the curriculum stipulated that she had to teach techniques, not creativity. She got along well with the enthusiastic schoolkids but hated having to call the parents when the kids were skipping class to go to KFC. After a couple of years she quit, and her mother hasn't forgiven her to this day. Now Lin dreams of receiving a grant to study art abroad, of being able to leave the country.

We reach the Red Brick Art Museum, a private art temple built, not surprisingly, almost completely out of red bricks. The current exhibition is called *The Unspeakable Openness of Things*, by the Islandic artist Olafur Eliasson, which is a series of light, water and mirror installations that each takes up one whole exhibition room.

I ask Lin, "Was the title intended to be political?"

"The police check every exhibition, but they don't see everything," she says, and laughs.

The installation with the same title as the exhibition certainly inspires speculation as to whether it has a hidden political message. In the middle of a room is a huge circle that appears to float but is actually a semicircle that gets its full shape from a mirror on the ceiling. The visitors, too, are reflected in the mirror. So far, so innocent. But everything is bathed in an orange tint that could be a reference to the color of the second-highest smog level warnings, which Beijing had reached numerous times in the previous months. Eliasson is well known for broaching ecological issues, and he seems to have achieved this here without being detected. Beijing visitors lie on the floor and look up at their reflections on the ceiling, enveloped in orange hues. Lin is visibly impressed.

We take a Didi cab (the Chinese equivalent to Uber) to the 798 Art Zone in the northeastern part of the city, where she is very keen to see an exhibition by a controversial American artist.

Beijing's most famous art district had a German past. In the 1950s, a delegation of East German architects, under the informal heading Project #157, planned a Bauhaus–inspired factory complex for electrical goods. Accommodation for twenty thousand workers was included in the design, and soon after opening, the complex was considered the best in all of China. The sound technology for the Workers' Stadium in Beijing and the loudspeakers for Tiananmen Square were built here, as well as electronics for military purposes. But in the 1980s, the factory began to lose its importance, whole departments were closed down and workers were laid off. The site was about to be demolished, but in 1995, artists moved in and turned the factory halls into studios.

Industrial ruins and contemporary art proved to be a good match, and 798 Art Zone became a huge success. In no time at all it became commercialized with product presentations from Sony and a Christian Dior store, souvenir shops, trendy restaurants and parking spaces for tourist buses.

The roads are flanked by thick metal tubing and sculptures. I discover a larger-than-life headless Mao suit; the artist who made it, Sui Jianguo, was one of the first artists to come here. A group of kids in skateboarder gear are taking selfies in front of a thirty-foot-high mural of King Kong smashing through a brick wall. A relaxed police officer lights a cigarette.

We ignore countless galleries as Lin heads directly to the M Woods Museum. The exhibition entitled *Innocence* presents video works by the Californian artist Paul McCarthy, who is famous for shaky B movies in which actors with grotesque rubber noses improvise all kinds of allusions to Disney characters, TV series and Grimms' fairy tales. The videos are deliberately disturbing because of the vast quantities of ketchup, mayonnaise and syrup that are used during the performances, because of the pissing and farting that goes on and because the director is evidently attempting to make the occasional pornographic moments appear not too erotic in any way.

McCarthy explores the limits of tolerance, and then merrily shows what is to be found beyond them. His *Painter* video ends with a scene in which an art critic drops in on an artist and, as a form of greeting, starts enthusiastically sniffing the artist's naked butt, as if this is a perfectly normal social interaction. And in *White Snow*, viewers witness Snow White participating in a two-hour orgy on the big screen with the seven dwarves. Lin endures the whole film; nobody else lasts to the final scene.

"Genius!" is her verdict.

So much crossing of borders, so much anti-aesthetics and anarchy—and all of it taking place in the middle of Beijing.

"The moral police were probably deceived by the fairy tale title and the word 'innocence' and didn't take a proper look," Lin suggests.

Maybe there are also different rules for well-known foreign artists and the locals. It is difficult to say whether the Chinese artists would be allowed to show such an exhibition. The regime is clever enough to not let its subjects know exactly where the red line is.

From: Qing Policewoman
Hello, how's it going? Where are you going next?

To: Qing Policewoman
Hangzhou and Yunnan. Going to drop by?

From: Qing Policewoman
Maybe to Guiyang? It's in the middle. Only five hours by
train for me

To: Qing Policewoman
No kidding? Okay!

From: Qing Policewoman
You do the organizing and I'll simply follow, okay? I need a
break

To: Qing Policewoman
Okay! I'll take care of things

From: Qing Policewoman
You're sounding very manly now haha

SCHNAPPI
IN SHANGHAI

ALL THE SCANDALOUS art in Beijing meant I had too little time to see the other attractions, but from my previous travels, I can report that the Forbidden City, the Temple of Heaven and the Summer Palace are all very much worth a visit.

For me, after saying farewell to Lin, the journey continues by express train to the southeast. A CRH380A bullet train travels the 819 miles from Beijing to Shanghai in four hours and twenty-eight minutes, at speeds of up to 208 miles per hour. There must be a strong fear of accidents along this route for it to need so many links to the lucky number eight. Eight is *ba* in Chinese and sounds very similar to the words for "advance" or "become wealthy."

Luckily, I'm not superstitious, as my train is number G4, and I am sitting in the fourth carriage, in seat 14F. The number four, *si*, sounds like the verb "to die" and is thought to bring bad luck. Many buildings don't have a fourth or fourteenth floor, many airlines don't have a seat four and no Chinese business would open a new branch on the fourth of any month. However, customers will pay high prices for phone numbers or car license plates with lots of eights, and the best day to marry is August 8. The organizers of the Olympic Games went one step further: the sporting event opened on August 8, 2008, at eight minutes past eight in the evening.

Despite the cluster of unlucky numbers, my train arrives on the dot. I take the subway to meet Ms. Wang, the "normal friend" of my visa application. After six weeks in China, I am finally where I was actually supposed to be the whole time, but fortunately, nobody had checked. Ms. Wang's first name is Huifen, and we know each other from two of my previous trips to China.

She lives in a building complex in a pretty corner of the former French Concession, a quarter with British pubs, German beer bars, Thai spas and French bakeries. Huifen is thirty-one, works as a Chinese teacher and is one of the most positive people I have ever met. In a country of constraints, she seems to be unencumbered, unhurried, and she is never serious for long. If something does go wrong, then it is somehow odd, so what's the point of working yourself up? Additionally, she has a passion for bright colors and pandas. Her two-room apartment is totally panda themed: here a cushion, there a fan, stuffed toys, fridge magnets, blankets and lollipops. Even the Q-tip pack in the bathroom is shaped like China's favorite animal, which simply doesn't seem to match the country at all. Pandas are lazy and vegetarian, two tendencies that most Chinese parents are certainly not fond of.

Speaking of which, Huifen's mother is visiting for a few days. She, too, exudes serenity to an extent that I have seldom

157

experienced in China and is miles away from the tiger mom stereotype. As a greeting, she plays a German song on her laptop, *"Schnappi das kleine Krokodil"* (Schnappi the Little Crocodile), and both mother and daughter sing along to the chorus while shimmying their shoulders. Huifen dances one of the toy pandas along the table.

After pinching myself on the arm a number of times just to make sure that I'm not dreaming, I ask them how they came across that song, which was a number one hit in Germany some years ago.

"You can often hear it here on online cooking shows," says Huifen. "No idea why."

Her mother is so pleased by my unmistakable bafflement that she clicks on the next song. On we go with yodel maestro Franzl Lang with *"Auf und auf voll Lebenslust,"* *"Eifersucht"* by Rammstein and *"Es ist ein Schnee gefallen,"* a flowery interpretation of a traditional folk song by a medieval rock group named Adaro. How did this unusual playlist come to be? Huifen's mother simply typed *"dewen yinyue"*—"German music"—into a Chinese video website and these were the first hits (you can find all of them on YouTube to get an idea). China's view of Germany distilled down to the lyrics of four popular songs.

The counterprogram is provided by an old man living next door. Huifen's love of pandas is matched by the neighbor's love for his karaoke computer program. With ample pathos, he begins singing about horses and the steppes. Despite the wall between us, we can easily hear everything.

158   "This happens almost every morning and every evening," says Huifen. She has to share a kitchen outside the apartment with him. "The times that he doesn't sing, he argues with his wife, which is why I prefer the singing."

"What do they argue about?" I ask.

"They argue nonstop, almost always about jealousy. He shouts stuff like: 'Just because that woman likes me, doesn't mean that I like her,' or 'I could have anybody!' The man is over seventy, his wife twenty years younger. I don't need a TV; that is the best soap opera ever."

Huifen is also linked to her neighbor via WeChat. He often posts photos and videos from karaoke bars, adding short messages like: "We're singing and dancing, very happy." Also thanks to WeChat, she knows that he used to work as a civil engineer and is probably well-to-do. He bought an apartment a couple of streets away in a good area.

Once, his door was wide open and he was standing in just his underpants in the living room, singing his heart out. From the floor above, a neighbor threatened to call the police because of the noise, but to no avail. Half an hour later, the singing stopped without the arrival of the police.

On another occasion, Huifen overheard a telephone conversation when his wife was not at home. "The man asked another woman if she wanted to cook for him, because, he said, 'My wife isn't a good cook.' Then he went on to praise the woman's singing—they must have met at some karaoke bar—adding: 'My wife can't sing.' A short while later, he left the apartment. He was probably going on a date with her."

We keep listening for a bit. You couldn't accuse him of lacking enthusiasm in his interpretations of Chinese hits, even though only every second note is in tune. In the songs, he imagines himself away, far away from his apartment; he is no longer a retired engineer in Shanghai but an adventurer in the grasslands of wildest Mongolia.

From: Qing Policewoman
I've booked accommodation in Guiyang!

To: Qing Policewoman
Super!

From: Qing Policewoman
Actually it isn't authorized for foreigners but we'll give it a go

From: Qing Policewoman
If you are not allowed to stay I will laugh a bit then find somewhere else for you hahaha

To: Qing Policewoman
Very funny! I thought I was supposed to do the organizing?

From: Qing Policewoman
Before traveling I always get nervous. I've also already booked something in a village. The Chinese can't relax ;)

A PENSIVE HULK

THE NEXT DAY I want to go to a stadium and watch some soccer. Huifen can't join me, but she has to go to the subway station, so we walk together for a while. Just outside the apartment complex we pass a massive touch screen with information for citizens: the location of the nearest police station, a map of the neighborhood showing nearby stores and businesses. It also displays local news, advertising films and clips of Shanghai citizens jaywalking. Their faces are recognizable so that everybody knows how easy it is to get into trouble.

A couple of steps farther, I wonder about a closed sliding window in the wall. Just one year ago, on my last visit, this was one of Shanghai's most popular ice cream parlors: WIYF. At the busiest times of the day, customers had to wait two to three hours to be served, standing in a line beneath plane trees that stretched all the way back to the next corner. "Homemade ice cream," "Delicious" and "All natural" can still be seen on the pastel-colored retro poster.

The owner, a Frenchman named Franck Pecol, had numerous other bistros and bakeries in the city and must have made a fortune. How could he give up such a successful business?

"Oh, there was a scandal. The whole city was talking about it," reports gossip-loving Huifen. "The bakeries were using sacks of flour that were months past the best by dates. And in one of the kitchens, rats were running around at night. A former employee exposed it by secretly filming it all and posting it on Weibo."

The boss fled to France, a number of employees were sent to prison and the shops closed.

"Economic success in China can be very short-lived," says Huifen.

However, the case was not totally undisputed, even though 578 sacks of dubious flour were seized. Online commentators discussed how dangerous the outdated flour actually was, the possibility the entrepreneur had enemies and what infractions would come to light if someone were to secretly film other bakeries.

I think about Huifen's neighbor and how she is privy to so much of his private life. I also think about the public screens showing offenders who crossed the road on a red light and the baker with the whistle-blower employee, not to mention the surveillance cameras on every corner. No matter where you are in China, in private or public, at work or leisure, you should not for a minute feel unobserved.

At the subway station, video cameras document us going our separate ways: Huifen to work and me to Shanghai Stadium. The turnout is relatively modest for today's game of Shanghai Shenhua against Beijing Renhe Football Club in the fifth round of the league cup. At the Shanghai Stadium stop, many people get off the train, but only two are wearing the soccer team's red jersey. There is a line of scalpers asking, "*Piaozi yao wa?*"—Shanghai slang for "Need a ticket?" They stretch from the subway exit all the way to the streets that surround the sports complex. Sometimes they want 380 yuan (fifty U.S. dollars), sometimes 100 or 80.

I brush them all off and look for the official ticket office—which isn't all that easy to find. There are no signs pointing the way, so I ask for directions at a hotel, at the team merch store and from two passersby. Twice I am pointed in the wrong direction, and twice the person I ask doesn't know. I seem to have discovered the only eighty-thousand-capacity stadium in the world without a ticket office. Did the architect forget it when designing the building?

So I turn to a scalper. He wants fifty yuan at first (seven dollars—the closer to kickoff, the cheaper the tickets seem to get). I say, "Thirty," and he says, "Forty." I say, "No thanks" and turn to go, so he shouts, "Thirty" at me. Agreed.

I'm not sure whether this ticket will work, but the policewoman at the entrance just chuckles, says, "*Laowai*" and waves me through. I step inside to find a huge oval with an awful lot of bucket seats and very few people. A beer would be helpful now to get into league cup mood, but alcohol is forbidden here. Instead, I buy two bone-dry muffins and tomato-flavored potato chips and take my $4.25 seat in block 18, row 35.

The players are displayed on a gigantic screen. Shanghai has two world stars on its team: the Brazilian international players Oscar and Hulk. Both were on the Brazilian team for their historic 1–7 loss to Germany in the 2014 FIFA World Cup, and it was even Oscar who scored the consolation goal. Two years later, he transferred from Chelsea to Shanghai for US$68 million and now earns US$460,000 a week. Surprisingly, he named unselfish reasons for transferring: "Of course the English league is stronger, but I'm here to help." Hulk (the nickname refers to his robust stature and style of play) cost the club US$65 million and earns US$400,000 a week. His huge headshot on the screen seems to be looking pensively at the empty seats. Maybe money isn't everything in an athlete's life. China, as shown by the huge transfer sums, has big plans for soccer. Something similar happened in 1950, when Mao declared that table tennis was to be the national sport, and now most world champions come from China. Mao was pretty shrewd to choose a discipline that wasn't particularly popular in the West and gave no particular advantage to the physically strong. Diving, badminton and gymnastics are other examples of sports where China regularly walks away with the gold medal. In soccer, however, China is seventy-three in the FIFA world rankings, between South Africa and North Macedonia.

Now Xi is saying that China will be the world champion in 2050. That could be taken as the babbling of a sixty-six-year-old dreamer who used to kick a soccer ball around at school, but the man is now head of state and all of a sudden there is a huge amount of money available for China's future favorite sport. Currently, there are twenty thousand soccer schools across the country; the largest, in Guangzhou, has room for three thousand young talented players. Also, soccer is being put on the school curricula throughout the country. Chinese companies are buying majority shares in top European clubs such as Inter Milan and Aston Villa, the Chinese Super League buys foreign players and coaches for vast sums of money. At the 2018 World Cup in Moscow, Chinese sponsors were so pervasive that visitors were constantly asking themselves what companies like Wanda, Vivo and Mengniu actually produce.

The Best Chinese Translations of Foreign Brand Names

1 Coca-Cola—*Ke kou ke le* ("tasty and makes you happy")

2 Reebok—*Rui bu* ("fast steps")

3 Viagra—*Wanaike* ("the guest who makes love ten thousand times")

4 BMW—*Bao ma* ("valuable horse")

5 Oral-B—*Ou le-B* ("European joy B")

But wait a minute: How is it possible that this patriotic government would hype such an obviously "Western" mass phenomenon? Yeah, right, they say here, soccer is Chinese anyway. Even in the third century BCE, they played *cuju*, a game similar to soccer, ages before English villagers first kicked a pig's bladder towards the next village's gateposts. Ideologically, it suits them, too, as yet another example of early Chinese advancement.

The practice of hiring international stars does, however, have its pitfalls. Carlos Tevez, for example, a thirtysomething Argentinian, jogged so sedately across the pitch for his US$554,000 a week that his coach at Shanghai Shenhua accused him of being too fat. After just a year with a mere sixteen appearances and four goals, he terminated his contract prematurely in 2018. Then the signing away of Cristiano Ronaldo didn't work out, even though one team was apparently offering US$330 million in transfer fees and an annual salary of US$110 million. Chinese Super League clubs have offered Robert Lewandowski, Arjen Robben and Pierre-Emerick Aubameyang absurd sums, but they all turned them down.

I can guess why from being at a cup game like the one today. Some five thousand spectators have sat down on red-and-gray bucket seats inside the huge oval grounds, roughly 0.02 percent of the city's population. "Walk for forever—endless dream" is written in quirky English on a red banner. It was probably trying to say: "We are not yet where we want to be." A few fans do, however, try to spur on their team with some chanting.

Shanghai begins with some bad luck—in the thirteenth minute, Oscar falls to the ground after challenging for a header and has to be substituted. Then follows a not particularly high-class game with plenty of bad passes, a bit of skirmishing in midfield and few chances of goals. Hulk wears yellow cleats and the yellow captain's armband; otherwise, he is only conspicuous because of one scene with a back heel pass and an attempt at goal from eighty feet that is only inches wide of the target. After ninety minutes, the score is 0-0, with no extra time being played but moving straight ahead with the penalty shoot-outs. And it is here that Hulk makes his most spectacular impact. Twice, he sets up the ball, takes nine steps back, makes a long run up, and then stops suddenly before shooting an unstoppable goal into the right corner. The following decisive penalty kick by the opponents is saved by Shanghai's goalie, and his team wins 4-3. The spectators clap politely but not unduly loudly.

Will China succeed as a future soccer superpower? I cannot divine the future from one game, but the enormous investment in young Chinese talent will soon spawn homegrown stars, and a few of them might become known internationally and win the country some Brownie points. The parallels to industrial advancement of recent years are interesting—there, too, China used foreign know-how, learned something new quickly and caught up at an incredible speed. The same could happen with soccer—and, in this case, without controversies about plagiarism or intellectual property.

INTERNET
CELEBRITY FACE

AT THE IN77 shopping mall in Hangzhou, A young woman in a lace dress sits in a shop window tapping away at a computer. She has white earbuds, a radio mic in front of her and a cell phone mounted on a tripod. Her desk is surrounded by stuffed animals. Behind her is a store selling perfume and lipstick in umpteen variations, with "A New Kind of Shopping" printed on the glass door. Next to and above the shop window you can see the face of the same woman, five times the real size, on a total of five upright video screens. Her video image has larger eyes and paler skin, and all her movements are shown with roughly half a second delay. Passersby can read her live conversations with online customers asking for product information and makeup tips or even hoping for a date (one guy promises, "I could please you for hours on end," but she ignores him). According to data in the top left corner, there are 13,376 internet viewers at the moment on the streaming platform Yizhibo. With fluttering eyelashes, the woman pleads for more likes, "so that we can be the hottest online store." It's like the shopping channel but more personal, like a sales call at home but with thousands of recipients at the same time, like a video call from a friend but with a commercial touch. How times change—a few years ago, people who sat nonstop in front of a computer were considered nerds, but nowadays, they can become stars.

My host, Pierre, welcomes me in the northeastern part of Hangzhou. He, too, dreams of being a *wang hong* face, a famous internet personality. "But not for my looks," he says. "I make comedy videos." He is twenty-four, wears black-rimmed glasses and has a table in his one-room apartment that is almost an exact copy of the lipstick marketing girl's workplace—microphone, cell phone tripod, monitor, plus a couple of fake books for decoration.

Pierre is tall and slim and belongs to the group of people who look totally different without their glasses: transforming from high school bookworm to teenage idol in a second. There is a video of him in which he complains about foreigners

169

who don't pay for admission to nightclubs and drink for free because the club owners believe that the more foreigners they get, the better it is for business. This, he declares, is unfair. The video got more than 4 million clicks.

"I exaggerated my face's digital optimization a bit, though. I still keep getting requests because of it from girls who want to get to know me. I write back telling them that in real life I'm not that good-looking," he says.

Later, I watch the videos; he looks almost exactly the same as he does in the flesh—but without glasses.

From: Qing Policewoman
Another thing I wanted to say: there is a rule

To: Qing Policewoman
What rule?

From: Qing Policewoman
No attempts at seduction. Hahaha

To: Qing Policewoman
Does that apply to me or you?

From: Qing Policewoman
You. You must keep yourself under control

To: Qing Policewoman
Whaaat??? But you can seduce me?

From: Qing Policewoman
Won't happen. Just pretend I'm your sister

Pierre knows all about image processing, because he works for a start-up firm making advertising campaigns for photographic software. In studio conditions he tries to get the most out of cell or drone cameras to show customers their potential. He can lecture for hours on camera types and technical data.

His favorite leisure activity also has something to do with entertainment technology. He writes in his Couchsurfing profile, as if it were a contradiction: "I love life. But I also love playing LoL." LoL is the abbreviation for *League of Legends*, the most popular online computer game in China. Two teams, each with five heroes, fight each other and try to destroy their opponent's HQ. Simple principle, incredible success: Today, there are national and international championships, with twenty thousand spectators at the final showdown, and the best gamers, thanks to lucrative advertising deals, can become quite wealthy. This is yet another variation of sitting in front of a computer and becoming famous.

But is it a dream for Pierre?

"No way! I'm far too old," he exclaims.

"You're twenty-four," I say.

"Yeah, but my reactions are already slower. Most gamers stop playing at twenty-three or twenty-four and do something else. Some of them already have permanent damage to their eyes or backs. Twelve or fourteen hours on the computer a day is not healthy."

He logs in to his profile to give me a crash course. "We play with four other people against AI, artificial intelligence. It's easier to begin with," he explains. "First, we have to choose our champion. Do you want to be an assassin, marksman or mage? An assassin causes maximum destruction, a marksman can attack from long distances and the mage—he uses magic, of course."

I choose assassin and a short while later a character materializes on the paved floor of a fantasy world of forests and towers, in which friends are marked green and foes red. If only things were that simple in real life. With the right mouse click Pierre moves the character, and with the Q, W, E and R keys he selects special weapons. He battles, runs, buys new weapons, attacks towers and defends against an "enemy rampage" with a "double kill." Everything is happening so quickly that, as a spectator, I feel way older than twenty-four.

Many of the game's announcements are in English, so you shouldn't be surprised if young Chinese people understand sentences like "Your inhibitor is respawning soon" or "An ally has been slain" better than those they learn in language classes. According to a 2018 study by the Ministry of Education, 18 percent of Chinese teenagers spend more than four hours a day playing computer games. The trend of escapism and enacting heroic deeds in fantasy worlds seems to be particularly well honed here. Some sociologists trace this back to a certain isolation that resulted from the one-child policy.

In 2008, China was the first country in the world to declare computer game addiction a psychological disorder that required therapy. At the same time, the government wants to foster a younger generation that is familiar with computer technology: in 2018, it added courses in artificial intelligence to the school curriculum. And, of course, China has nothing against the economic success that local game producers have garnered. Their $28 billion industry that grew thanks to the huge demand is now the largest market globally.

But, still, there are controversies about individual games, such as the enormously popular *Honor of Kings*, a relative of *LoL* specially designed for mobile devices. The potential for addiction is thought to be so high that the makers, Tencent, have been forced to introduce a mechanism for blocking play after an hour for minors. A case in Hangzhou caused a stir after a thirteen-year-old argued with his dad about his gaming habit, ran way and jumped from a building, breaking both legs. The young man believed that he could fly, like some of his *Honor of Kings* characters.

There are thought to be 23 million gaming addicts in China. The authorities have passed stricter laws and introduced boot camps with military drills and corporal punishment in an attempt to lead young people to a more virtuous path.

Pierre has his doubts about whether this really helps. "Constant updates and new characters make it difficult to stop. Once you start, it's not so easy to escape," he says, while hitting the Q key energetically, making the brave assassin blast a number of opponents simultaneously. "'Double kill,'" says the computer approvingly.

· · · · · · · · ·

BACK TO THE real world. "In Heaven there is paradise and on Earth there is Hangzhou and Suzhou," goes the Chinese saying. The merchant and explorer Marco Polo even said of Hangzhou, "this city is the most beautiful and greater than any in the world" because the markets and canals reminded him of Venice and West Lake enchanted him.

The markets have become malls and the canals have become streets. But the lake is still there, surrounded by sumptuous parks and woods. This is a spectacular amount of green space for a metropolis of 9.8 million in China, where trees in an attractive location need pretty good arguments not to be declared, sooner or later, obstacles to progress.

The air is sticky, the sky cloudy and the water not as blue as on the Photoshopped postcards of Hangzhou. Still, or maybe because of it, this lake, with its green meadows, red lotus flowers on its banks and picturesque pavilions and bridges, has a melancholic magic. In some places it is even possible not to have a single skyscraper in view, and the water, which is on average only five feet deep, seems to be moderately clean. Efforts to remove algae and chemicals took many years before the mayor could finally ceremoniously announce: "If you fill a bottle of water here, it looks just like mineral water!"

The Best Chinese Bottled Water

1   Ganten—hardly any aftertaste, nice bottle design, a lovely little drop of water

2   Alkaqua—sounds like the name of a digestif but is non-alcoholic and has a pleasing and relatively neutral taste

3   C'est Bon—means "It's good" or "Okay" in French; here, it's the latter

4   Nongfu Spring—one of the biggest brands in China. A strong chlorine aftertaste suggests that great chemical efforts were needed to make it drinkable

5   Wahaha—funny name, unfunny taste; something like the water from the local outdoor swimming pool

The most famous city legend tells us what else lurks in West Lake. A white snake with magical powers once slid out of the lake near the Broken Bridge and morphed into the form of a woman so pretty that she immediately found a young gentleman named Xu Xian who would offer her his umbrella when some raindrops started to fall. They exchanged WeChat details (or what did they do back then?) and decided to marry and open an apothecary. Eternal marital bliss seemed assured, until a swamp turtle with an aversion to snakes crawled out of the lake and morphed into the form of a monk and planned to show poor Xu what he had actually married. The turtle monk made the snake lady drink a beaker of enchanted realgar wine at the next Dragon Boat Festival, and, hey, presto, *in vino veritas*, her real species was revealed. Xu overreacted, dying of shock.

But lucky is the man married to a clever, newly widowed apothecary. She remembered a magic stimulant, a herb she picked on the slopes of Mount Emei, that would restore him to life. The freshly awoken one declared her snake-likeness to be not so bad and claimed that he just died in the heat of the moment, a moment of surprise that won't happen again. To emphasize his words, Xu impregnated his rescuer—and not a moment too soon, as a short while later the mean monk rang the doorbell, kidnapped him and locked him up in a monastery. An attempt to free him by the loyal apothecary with the swelling belly went wrong, but eventually, he managed to escape, became a father and witnessed his snakelady wife become imprisoned in the Leifeng Pagoda—never a dull moment. She was kept there for decades, until she could finally be freed. The family was reunited, the monk fled to hide in the stomach of a crab and, to this day, hardly anyone comes

175

to the Broken Bridge or to Leifeng Pagoda without thinking about this love story.

The five-story pagoda was once the victim in another legend. It was said that its stones were a defense against evil spirits and helpful for the birth of male offspring. The pagoda collapsed in 1924 because too many visitors took stones as keepsakes. In 2002, the old symbol of the city was reconstructed true to the original on its hill by the lakeshore, where it is now surrounded by enough cameras to ensure nobody takes away any of its stones.

"Tourist density crowded" is on the screen by the ticket office—sounds like they think of tourists as a mass, not as individuals. The information is just stating the obvious since it is May 1, a national holiday that draws a big crowd. The visitors come in single file on winding wooden walkways along the shore, and hundreds wait at the steps to the pagoda; from above, they must look like white snakes in their light T-shirts and caps. Here and there you can see a wedding gown because the romantic setting is very popular for wedding photographs. Men dressed in tailor-made suits and patent-leather shoes and women with thirty-foot trains pose for pictures. The air is murky and the water grim, but with a little retouching, it will all look fantastic.

To: Qing Policewoman
Do I go into the hotel alone if I arrive before you?

From: Qing Policewoman
If you're clever, yes

From: Qing Policewoman
开智能锁密码；039858#
你们到了贵阳北站上到西广场可看到西广场对面的楼顶几个大字；北大资源梦想城，梦园公寓就在这一楼盘的A02栋楼，你们走到亚朵酒店大门口，可见正对面有一红色滚动字幕；梦想酒店从此上四楼，你们也从此门进入电梯间，上到12楼，出电梯右转走走廊左边第二间就是12/05号房。开智能锁方法；用手盖住门手把之上的数字频，手往下一划，数字显现，操作密码，完成后数字频左上角出现时，搬动门手把，门打开。

To: Qing Policewoman
Shit

From: Qing Policewoman
Okay: Building A02, 12th floor, pass code 039858. I'll send you directions via Baidu maps

NOT AS BAD
AS HITLER

AFTER AN EIGHT-HOUR journey of more than a thousand
miles (these high-speed trains rock!), I reach the enormous station at Guiyang. The capital of Guizhou province
has a population of 4.7 million, so in the U.S. it would be the
second-most populous city, between New York and Los Ange-
les. Nevertheless, outside China, hardly anyone knows of
it, though recently it has become a very important center of
technology. Foreigners seldom come here, but their data does.
Since February 2018, everyone with an iPhone registered on
Apple's Chinese iCloud services is using the gigantic server
operated by Guizhou-Cloud Big Data Industry Development
(GCBD), a company under government control. In the general
terms of business, a small but not insignificant sentence states:
"Apple and GCBD have the right to access...all user data including content." It is hardly surprising, then, that foreign tech
blogs recommend not registering on Chinese iCloud.

The locals, however, don't have this option. Even technology giants such as Alibaba, China Mobile, China Telecom and Huawei store their user data in Guiyang. Big Data Valley, an important foundation for the super-networked, all-observing future of the country, evolved in a relatively underdeveloped province, of all places, where more than half the population lives below the poverty line.

My map app directs me to the station forecourt, where soldiers are practicing a drill, and then via a pedestrian underpass to the other side of the road. My destination is a high-rise with a noodle soup restaurant on the ground floor. In the elevator there is an ad for a luxury massage parlor and one for an online used car lot, xin.com, which courts customers with a picture of Leonardo DiCaprio. I do some research later and discover it is an official advertising partnership, not just a picture stolen from the internet. The U.S. superstar demoted to a car dealer—sometimes it is the minor details that show how the world is changing.

179

I get out of the elevator at the twelfth floor. The code works, and I enter a tidy twin room with a large bathroom and massive windows with a view of the skyline. Twenty dollars a night for perfect comfort. Qing immediately wins bonus points as a good trip planner. I go back to the station to meet her, and it is already dark and beginning to rain.

From: Qing Policewoman
Just arrived

From: Qing Policewoman
West Square exit?

To: Qing Policewoman
Yes. I'm at the end of the hall

From: Qing Policewoman
Impossible to miss you, you're six foot

To: Qing Policewoman
Hao a

From: Qing Policewoman
Please, no Chinese

To: Qing Policewoman
Wei shenme?

From: Qing Policewoman
Because I have to laugh at you

Soon I see her heading towards me, a bright speck in the middle of a heavy flow of passengers. She is wearing a sky-blue jacket, white pants and white shoes.

"I'm tired. Last night I was on night shift," she says by way of greeting.

"Supper is on me. Up for sour fish soup?"

"Sure! My favorite food in Guiyang!" Her gloomy expression brightens. "Respect. You know everything."

"What do you mean 'everything'?"

"You know what the best dish in Guiyang is. That's pretty much everything."

"You are very Chinese," I say, and then we get into a cab.

In the dark, a faceless city flashes by, drab high-rises and the usual illuminated signs of restaurants and convenience stores. Hanging from a wall are blue posters with propaganda slogans promoting the new digital world: "Big Data—Blockchain—Bright Prospects," "Digital Economy Prompts New Growth," and "Use Big Data for Social and Economic Development."

The bit about growth is true. According to a report from *Sixth Tone*, by Zhejiang University sociology professor Li Jing, an incredible sixteen thousand new tech companies and 155 research institutes registered in Guiyang in the first six months of 2018 alone.[12] Other things are being tested here, too, such as a particularly efficient surveillance system for catching criminals. "Guiyang has 'Skynet' everywhere; wherever you go, you will be watched," claims the local police department's press release. Skynet is the massive centralized video surveillance network that compares face recognition data with passport photos of Chinese citizens, and analyzes GPS data and car movements. Qing, from the high-tech city of Shenzhen, should feel at home here.

I hope she doesn't get into trouble because of it.

"Actually, I should get authorization from my employers when I travel to a different province. But it's a hassle. You have to state reasons, and often they won't allow you to take the whole time span, so I skipped it," says my favorite policewoman.

Our feast is to be served on the second floor of an inconspicuous shopping mall in the Old Kaili Sour Fish Restaurant. The staff wear traditional colorful outfits and jingling silver headdresses of the Miao ethnic group. Qing chooses a fish from an aquarium in a neighboring room that will shortly be served in broth in an octagonal metal pot. Red chilies are swimming on the soup's surface, little fortune-tellers with the message: "Your tongue is about to burn and you will be thankful for it."

"I usually don't like spicy food, but last time I was here I had fish soup three days in a row. Simply too good," says Qing.

The table is almost bending under the weight of the side dishes: green salad, spring onions, slices of carrot, vegetables wrapped in rice paper and baked tofu balls. On the first bite, I am reminded of Henry Kissinger—or rather, a quotation: "After a dinner of Peking duck, I'll sign anything," the former top U.S. diplomat is reported to have once said, and I am certain that in Guiyang he would extend his praise to include this delicious fish soup. The cheesy Mandopop coming from the speakers, the clattering of cutlery and the discussions around us create constant background noise.

Qing and I chat about cuckoo clocks and Adolf Hitler. Qing would love to buy a cuckoo clock if she ever to went to Germany. She refuses to accept my subtle hints that it isn't a suitable lifestyle addition for someone in her youthful age bracket, or that after a couple of days the acoustic charms might begin to lose their appeal: "I want one!" she insists. In China, the line separating what is usual at what age is different. Twenty-year-olds hang cuckoo clocks on the wall, forty-year-olds carry Hello Kitty handbags and seventy-year-olds dance to Lady Gaga in the park. We end the subject with my suggestion that she should download a cuckoo clock app on a trial basis, which would save her a lot of money.

We land on Hitler after she asks about entry regulations for Germans visiting China. She thinks the maximum of a four-week stay with a standard tourist visa is pretty short.

"Do you think that it might have something to do with your history?" she asks.

"With our what?"

"Well, with Hitler and stuff."

"That was eighty years ago."

The diligent waitress tops up our bowls with hot soup from the huge pot between us.

"Do you think there is a reason why Hitler was possible in Germany, and not in another country? Or was it just coincidence?"

"There were a number of factors: the economic situation, the defeat of the First World War, his populist rhetoric."

"Maybe it was also because you are control freaks? Are Germans obsessive?"

"What do you mean?"

"Hitler had this idea of killing all Jews because he was an obsessive type. He couldn't bear the thought of a single survivor. I thought about Hitler because yesterday I killed all the mosquitos at my workplace."

"And...that made you feel like Hitler?" I ask, offended.

"Yes. I used this electronic flyswatter. There were so many! I've got bites everywhere. I couldn't bear to allow even one survivor. Then I went from one room to the next, killing them all."

Her line of thought makes me wonder if it also shows an obsessive character if a government wants to observe every single citizen 24-7. But I don't say it out loud.

"I'm becoming a bit afraid of you now," I say instead.

"But there is a difference between me and Hitler, right? He killed humans, and I kill mosquitoes, right? Mosquitoes are bad, right?"

"I'm going to say something to you that I've never said to a woman: you are not as bad as Hitler."

She laughs.

When a competition is held somewhere for the compliment of the year, I would like to enter that sentence.

. . . .

QING IS SATISFIED with the hotel room. Excellent affordability, separate beds and a good neighborhood, only a few minutes by foot to the station from which we plan to visit the villages the next day.

"Surely, you're always doing this, aren't you?" she asks, while putting on a moisturizing mask that makes her look like a ghost.

"What?"

"Inviting any pretty woman on your travels?"

"No, I'm very choosy."

"Ha ha ha, I don't believe a word. Just keep your hands to yourself."

Then she lies down and writes a few messages before taking off her mask and turning out the light.

It's very quiet in this well-insulated room on the outskirts of Guiyang, so quiet and dark. But all of a sudden, I'm somewhere else: in a pedestrian zone. I look around and wonder why everyone is wearing cylindrical headgear made of an opaque kind of glass, like old-fashioned welding masks with those murky little windows. At the top, the current scores are displayed: green for good, red for bad, and some are even black; other passersby stay well clear of those ones. On the sides of the headgear individual names are visible with information about work, health, awards, party membership and monthly wages. Whenever someone wins action points, there is a sound like the descending third of a cuckoo clock but slightly distorted, like in a computer game from the eighties. The points appear briefly in a red star in front of the person's face, with an explanation: a donation, an ecological accomplishment, a report of a criminal act.

A girl who looks like Qing but twenty years younger cheerfully translates the Chinese characters, saying that this technology has finally made the dream of a perfect society possible. Her own score is in the green range.

"Here, try this on," she says, and then somberly places one of the headgears on me, as if in a crowning ceremony.

Inside the headgear the air tastes sweet and smells like bubble gum; an air filter is part of the equipment. Suddenly, I see the world around me as if it were on a giant cell phone screen, where I can highlight individual points using my line of vision and blinking. I can see how much I have in common with passersby, that the guy on my left, just like me, likes playing guitar. An arrow on the ground shows where I can buy hiking boots—big sale, just two hundred yards away.

The program asks whether I want to post a status update on the outside of the cylinder, like: "Seeking work," "Looking for a girlfriend" or "Apartment for sale." I notice that everyone is walking at exactly the same pace and nobody is in danger of collision. Looking closer at my screen, I can see predetermined footsteps that I can follow like a player in a Wii dance video game. All those people are now players on a Wii dance game; nothing can happen to them if they follow the prearranged steps. Trying to gain more and more points could actually be fun, so much fun that at night you wouldn't even want to...

"Sleep," says young Qing.

"You can't sleep either?" is the whole sentence, and it comes from six feet to my left. All of a sudden I'm back in reality, lying in a hotel bed.

"What? Oh, no," I lie drowsily.

"Shall we watch a movie?" Qing asks.

I touch my head—no cylindrical headgear.

"How late is it?" I ask.

"Two-ish."

"Okay, fine."

She clambers across to my bed, leans her cell phone against a pillow in front of us and searches online for English movies. She finds an episode of the British comedy series *Horrible Histories*, which is all about the Vicious Vikings, the Rotten Romans and the Terrible Tudors. It's an alliterative view of world history that is probably wildly funny, but I find it hard to focus on the plot because whoever breaks the twin bed separation rule is actually signaling that the previously agreed upon brother/sister nonsense is possibly renegotiable.

186

When the cell phone falls to the floor, we don't even bother looking for it. Just how forbidden is all this? I am not allowed to be here because it is not a hotel for foreigners, and because Guiyang isn't in my visa. She is not allowed to be here because her trip hasn't been authorized, and she has a husband and child in Shenzhen. None of that matters now. In this room, we are invisible to the ten thousand cameras in the city; we are a mistake in the system, hidden from Skynet in a blind spot. From the floor rise the screams of Vikings and Roman gladiators as the *Horrible Histories* carry on without us.

· · · · · · · · · ·

A LITTLE BIT delirious but not unhappy, the next morning we get on the K112 train to Kaili, and then change at the sparkling-clean station to an e-bus to the villages. I gaze out the window and Qing taps away at her cell phone.

"This is really annoying. I have to confirm that I've read all of Xi Jinping's recent speeches," she says grumpily, and points at the screen.

The header graphics indicate that it's an official document, and it shows the entrance to the Forbidden City in Beijing and a *huabiao*, a ceremonial column with two wings and a mythical being at the top. People used to believe that the creature with a camel's head and a lion's mane notified the gods about their mood, like a kind of ancestor of the surveillance technology of today.

"I never read the speeches. I simply click them away," Qing admits. "So, another four and I'll be done."

Then she turns her attention to the online shop for police uniforms where she has vouchers worth around $270 every year. She orders socks and pajamas.

The Best Chinese Cell Phone Features

1 The popular online game *Clap for Xi Jinping* shows an excerpt of a speech by the state president, and then you have eighteen seconds to applaud as enthusiastically as possible by manically tapping the screen.

2 The flirting app Tantan can tell you how often you were at the same place at the same time as your current crush.

3 On the Miao A app, you can buy time with a celebrity. Everything from a WeChat message to a personal meeting is possible, depending on the size of your wallet.

4 WeChat users can post a kind of message in a bottle—note something you have always wanted to say anonymously there for other users to read.

5 With an app called Didi DaRen, you could hire a heavy to beat up your enemy. It was quickly withdrawn from the market once the media got wind of it.

Qing and I leave the small city, passing green mountains behind green synthetic netting and two impressive new buildings, both roughly fifteen stories high with a 160-foot facade. The snow-white front of the first building has a slogan about "Big Data" on it, and the second has beige walls and houses the law courts.

"They are intentionally built to radiate power," says Qing, having noticed my interest. "Just to tell the people: 'You'd better be careful, or else.'"

"Why are the Chinese so unconcerned about surveillance?" I ask.

"Its goal is to improve the quality of people. And that's a good thing. Besides that, we're used to being under surveillance from childhood on. My parents still keep an eye on me, even today. It's annoying, but they mean well." She points to the hemispheric cameras on the bus's ceiling. "And they are there to protect us. Have you heard of Yingying Zhang, the Chinese student who was murdered in the U.S.?"

"No."

"The main suspect denied everything, and it took more than two years for him to be convicted, because there are too few cameras in the USA. They still haven't found her body. This would be impossible in China. It is difficult for us to understand how this could happen in such a modern country as the U.S."

"But if someone is murdered at home or in the mountains, then, even here, there might be no clear evidence," I say.

"But you can see two people going into the house or to the mountains together, and whether they both come back. That's

189

pretty strong evidence. That's why we feel safe. And plenty of foreigners who come here do, too. Or are you scared?"

"Not of being mugged but rather of what happens to my data."

She makes a dismissive gesture. "It's no big deal. Although while I was training, I had a boss who watched me on the security monitors. He would suddenly summon me and said things like: 'You've just eaten an apple. Why didn't you offer me a bite?' On another occasion he tried to grope me. I was too young and naïve to tell anyone. Still, I'm more afraid in foreign countries than I am here."

"Why's that?"

"In Italy or France, Chinese tourists are often robbed. Many people who've been there advise against going out after dark. In China, that's not a problem."

"No narrow alleyways in the suburbs where you wouldn't go?"

"No, normally we're at home by 11:00 PM anyway. If it's later, we take a cab."

"In Europe, that's a pretty safe way of operating, too."

"I doubt it. Not in Italy or France. And certainly not in the USA, with all those weapons."

"Have you been to those countries?"

"No, I'd panic because I'm so small: five-foot-three, only an inch above the minimum height for policewomen. It'd be too easy to attack me."

Her idea of Western countries is probably not more inaccurate than most Westerners' concept of China. Most news reports and articles about China emphasize the bizarre, the extreme and the huge differences. But these stories are only one part of the truth.

In some regards, the developments in the Western world are not as different from China as we would like to think. We criticize China's state-supported mania for collecting data but continue our daily use of Facebook and Google, both of which store data and are more powerful than quite a few countries. We are frightened of dictatorships but are currently experiencing a renaissance of populism and authoritarian leadership. We are shocked by state-sponsored manipulation of opinions but have yet to find a way to combat foreign propaganda campaigns that are trying to spread misinformation to influence public opinion. We are skeptical of topics like total surveillance but have to ask ourselves to what extent are we willing to ignore the technological options available for something like crime prevention.

The bus has been following a river for quite some time now, and the villages are becoming smaller and look more traditional. The piles of concrete on the far riverbank, the precursors of a new railway line, look like an ugly intrusion of modernity. Qing describes a TV program about police work in which, thanks to the most advanced technology, the thieves and murderers are caught within minutes of their crimes. This is how propaganda works: inside the country, prime examples of the benefits of surveillance, and from abroad, reports about attacks on Chinese tourists.

We get out at the picturesque village of Jidao, walk down to the river and cross a bridge to reach our homestay. We hear the sound of trumpets and see a group of locals coming slowly towards us. The women have their hair done up in small balloon-like buns and are wearing bright clothing; the men are wearing blazers and cloth pants. In the middle, some men are bearing a wooden coffin covered in pink cloth towards the boundary of the village. 191

"He was only fifty but seriously ill," says our host, an elderly woman in a traditional Miao outfit who also has an impressive bun. "Six pigs were slaughtered today in his honor."

We deposit our backpacks in a tidy room with plenty of light-colored wood, push the twin beds together and then set off on a hike through the woods to the next village: Langde.

On arrival, Qing is surprised to discover that there is an entrance fee of sixty yuan (US$8.50). The last time she was here it was free. She asks a local if there is any way around paying the fee.

"Just go to the other entrance to the village and come in from there. I don't know why it costs something to enter—it's just a village," he answers cheerfully. "Do you want to have a drink with me? I'm looking for drinking companions!" He has slightly wayward, glassy eyes, and we politely decline his invitation.

We skirt around the village for a couple hundred yards and enter from the other side. We pass silver stores, quaint old houses and a venue for public dance events, and then head to a restaurant with simple wooden tables. It is a little early for dinner, but the owner says he is prepared to cook for us. On the wall is the obligatory kitchen grading by the hygiene authorities: a somewhat unhappy-looking smiley face doesn't seem to match a B grade. Taking a closer look, I notice that it was pasted over an inferior C grade. Instant karma—visitors who skimp on the entrance fee are, in return, fleeced at supper.

You often hear that nobody trusts anybody in China, and I'm beginning to understand why. Qing says that online fraud is a huge problem. "Recently, my best friend wrote on WeChat that he had no money in his cell phone account and asked if I could quickly transfer two hundred yuan [thirty dollars] to him. Luckily, I didn't do it, as his account had been hacked."

We have time to talk, as the cook takes an eternity to rustle up a meal consisting of a bit of rice, some vegetables and some pork. Outside, a chicken wanders by, as do some kids wearing old-fashioned pants with open crotches that make diapers unnecessary—practical, but they do have disadvantages.

"Scams also happen without the internet," says Qing. "For example, a lot of old folks buy fake medication that claims to make you live to a hundred. They believe what is promised at shady advertising events. First, they are offered lots of free tests—blood pressure and so on. The waiting room is like a meeting place for seniors, with people chatting pleasantly. And the young staff in their doctor's getup look like perfect sons and daughters and are super friendly. Some of the old folks know that they are being cheated, but they don't think it's so bad because it feels nice to speak to these people."

After an age, the owner manages to place a warm bottle of Snow beer on the table.

"Shall I help you in the kitchen?" offers Qing, but her assistance is grumpily rejected.

"My mom was a victim of a fraud," she continues. "She was really stupid, I'm sorry to say." Qing's mother, who is anything but fond of traveling, suddenly announced that she was going to fly to Taiwan soon; indeed, the trip was apparently by invitation from the government there for her entire square dancing group. The patron of the enterprise was supposed to be none other than a grandson of former president Chiang Kai-shek.

"Old people have this romantic idea of Taiwan as an island of miracles that is naturally part of China, like a missing member of the family. We love Taiwan, and Taiwan loves us—that's what we learn in school."

Qing asked about the route, but her mother didn't know. 193 "However, she had already paid the money to some woman, not an agency. I was very suspicious. I advised her to ask about the route and to threaten to demand a refund."

But the operators refused to repay anything. "They even told her: 'You are the black sheep here. Everyone else is looking forward to the trip, and you're causing trouble. It is an honor to be invited by the government of our sister country!'"

This story reminds me of the other mother, the mother of Lin, the artist in Beijing. Her argument with her daughter sounded similar: people who step out of line are wrong; a good nail doesn't stick out.

"Mom's money was gone. Of course, she could have simply stayed at home, but she didn't want to let the scammers win," says Qing.

So she would rather go along and try to enjoy it somehow. Immediately on arrival at Taipei airport, however, it became apparent that something wasn't right. The promised official reception didn't take place; instead, the tour guide held up his cell phone, played a recorded trumpet fanfare and said a few nice words. The group had supposedly been invited to a grand banquet, and everybody was dressed up for it, but then there was no one there except their group. They went to a "famous local restaurant" that offered only substandard cold food.

"And they had paid the price of a luxury trip. They never saw a government representative. So funny."

Our food finally arrives after more than forty minutes. It doesn't taste particularly good.

"I'm going to give this restaurant a bad review," says Qing.

· · · · · · · · ·

194 CHINESE TOUR OPERATORS treat old villages like start-ups. They build little ticket booths, employ staff and encourage restaurateurs, store owners and hoteliers from elsewhere to set up shop there. A small share of the entrance money, maybe

5 percent, goes to the villagers. The rest finances renovations, with shares paid to the provincial government, and sometimes a little bribe to a particularly enterprising village councillor. However, the lion's share goes to the investor.

If hordes of visitors come, then it is a gold mine; if not, then the investor will swiftly move on, dismantling the ticket booth, and the village must once again cope alone.

"I don't think Langde will last that long. There are more famous villages with better attractions nearby. Why should people want to come here?" says Qing.

We hitchhike back to our accommodation with the young driver of a sand transporter. "Truckers are perfect for a lift," says traveling pro Qing. "They are bored with their routine, and they are not afraid of being robbed because everyone knows that they hardly earn anything."

The next morning Qing has bad news. An important meeting at work has been arranged spontaneously and she has to travel back earlier than planned, so we have just one more day. She suggests going back to the city.

"We can do that," I say. "Would you like to take a look at the new high-tech amusement park?"

"No."

"It's supposed to be amazing—the largest virtual reality park in the whole world."

"Sounds super boring."

She does a bit of online research. "Visitors say that a lot of attractions aren't open yet, that you have to wait four hours for two minutes on a roller coaster and that the entrance fee is expensive."

"I will pay for both of us."

"Go there alone."

"That's stupid. We have such little time left."

"Then let's go to a karaoke bar."

"I can't sing."

The discussion continues for a few minutes, until one of us finally gets their way.

A few hours later, we are walking through Guiyang searching for KTV establishments. The first candidate has a spectacular entrance made of fake marble and a smartly dressed elevator boy who brings us in an elevator full of golden mirrors to the first floor, where two heavily made-up ladies in miniskirts are standing behind a small bar. Sadly, there is no room for another two singers, they tell us.

"You could sing with one of the women, or if you pay a bit more, you could even take her home," says Qing, my China explainer.

In the neighborhood there are a number of karaoke bars, each with their own enticing slogan, from "Music: the end-less drink" (Man KTV) to "Happy every day" (Xin Chang KTV). Qing finds a good online offer for the former: 168 yuan (twenty-five dollars) for four hours, including eight bottles of beer and snacks.

A staff member escorts us to cabin A52. On the yellowish wooden wall hangs an expressionistic print of a saxophonist and a cellist in an oversized silver frame. There is a long black leather couch and, on the table next to a dice shaker, two mics with red and a blue LED lights on a golden base. A waiter knocks and brings in a tray full of sliced melon, cocktail tomatoes and filleted fish, a huge bucket of popcorn and eight bottles of Snow beer. On the wall, there are two screens: a smaller one for song selection and a larger one for the sing-along videos.

Qing starts off singing along with plenty of echo and lots of gusto to a Teresa Teng classic: "The Moon Represents My Heart."

To simulate the effect Teresa has on her audience, take an injection of custard in the arm, then fill a swimming pool with plenty of cotton candy and get in. While sinking deeper and deeper into the pink sugary goo, eat half a marshmallow cake. In other words, much as you would like to, it is impossible to resist the tempting sugariness of this song; at some point, it will suck you in, plant itself in your head and never leave.

The imagery and the quality of the video are less convincing, but after every line, a live overlay gives an evaluation of how precise the length and pitch of the singer's tone were. "Good" or "perfect" is faded in, or "combo ×3," or "combo ×4" when a number of verses worked out well. At the end, there is a digitally determined percentage—anything over 80 is pretty good, and above 90 is excellent.

Luckily, this function isn't available for the English songs. The reverb is the acoustic equivalent of exaggerated digital photo optimization—it makes every voice sound twenty-five years younger. I have a go at "Wonderwall," "Lemon Tree" and "Moon River"—the selection is not particularly extensive. Searching for a song is complicated because it takes me a while to understand the logic of the system. You have to type

197

in not the song title but rather the initials, so "WAY" for "We Are Young" or "BR" for "Bad Romance."

Thanks to the beer, and Qing's company, it is a wonderful evening, overshadowed by the fact that our time together is coming to an end; tomorrow she must return, and afterwards we will not meet again. After all, she has a husband and child in Shenzhen, and I won't be flying back to China in the foreseeable future. So this is to be our farewell, in the kitschy atmosphere of cabin A52, with melon snacks and watery beer and songs about eternal love.

. . . .

THE NEXT MORNING I take her to the station, and the I am alone again. What should I do to protect myself against the wrench of farewell? Virtual distraction and escape to fantasy worlds, what else? So it's off to the edge of town, to Oriental Science Fiction Valley!

I take a cab there and walk across a construction site to get to the entrance, where a staff member in a light blue uniform scans my ticket. I marvel at an over-150-foot-high Transformers figure and race through the night of a future city in a flying car. Then I get stuck in a carriage. In my virtual reality headset I can only see a sinister room from which there seems to be no escape—definitely not the experience that the ambitious high-tech city of Guiyang wishes to present to its guests. Just as I am considering getting out of the carriage and walking along the track to the door, my vehicle judders into motion. A couple of yards farther on, it stops again. On the screen of my glasses I can read an error prompt that I can close by blinking my eyes. And then I'm back in the room with the gray walls. What a miserable place to sit and think about how I'm missing Qing.

After what feels like an eternity, the carriage starts moving again, and this time, it actually reaches the door. I'm back in the real, illusory world, the one planned by park designers, with smiling staff members, bright-colored lights and spaceship-like buildings.

The sun peeps out from behind the clouds, happy families lick their ice cream and a wide-eyed kid unpacks the robot his dad bought him. At the roadside, cyborgs stand silently observing the happy goings-on.

The place that is best suited to drag me back from the future to the present is the old station in the center of Guiyang. Next to the main road and a bit below, beneath a hodgepodge of electric cables, is a dingy alleyway with thirteen-yuan (two-dollar) all-you-can-eat stands that smell of cheap fat, palm readers, massage parlors and, along the darkest stretch (sixty feet without any electric lighting at all) sex workers in filthy doorways to rooms you just don't want to think about.

I have a long journey ahead of me, so I buy some digestive cookies, "soft French bread" (more plastic packaging than bread), peanuts, two cans of Tsingtao beer, a 1.555-liter bottle of C'est Bon water and pickled paprika-beef instant noodles in a cardboard container. A word to the wise: never buy the cheapest instant noodles on the shelf; the extra thirty cents are well spent. Also, beware of packages with cartoons of crying or sweating chilies. With my provisions in plastic bags, I head for my platform.

Log of a Largely Uneventful
Train Journey From Guiyang to Kunming

6:02 PM

Seat 68 in car 17 located. The travel experiment can begin—booked the slowest connection between Guiyang and Kunming, almost eleven hours for 396 miles, night train, cheapest seating category. The seats are hard and the windows look as if they were last cleaned during the Ming dynasty.

6:09 PM

The K433 rolls punctually out of the station. Opposite: two young men, mid-twenties. One of them offers me pink chewing gum that I gratefully accept.

6:13 PM

On seat 54, a tanned man works on his cheeks with an electric razor, as if to say that it's perfectly natural to shave at 6:13 PM on the K433.

6:15 PM

The woman in seat 62 is transporting a curtain rail in her hand and wearing track pants that are exactly the same color as the chewing gum in my mouth. She knows nothing of the coincidence, and I refrain from pointing it out.

6:24 PM

A fruit seller treks along the aisle and offers, "*Wu kuai liang bao*"—two bags for five yuan (seventy-five cents). Nobody buys anything, and there is no visible indication on his face of whether he is particularly disappointed or not.

6:31 PM

Another mobile gastronomy vendor makes an attempt with rice, vegetables, meat and two boiled egg halves presented on polystyrene plates. "Hao chi—good food," he says, but that is not the first thing that comes to the mind of an objective observer.

6:52 PM

A number of fires, fortunately beyond the tracks—outside, burning bales of hay can be seen.

6:56 PM

"How much did your camera cost?" asks the chewing gum donor opposite. He is better dressed than me. "Eight thousand yuan," I answer. This is not the truth; it was considerably more expensive than eleven hundred U.S. dollars.

6:57 PM

His name is Wang Yahong, and his next questions are: "Where did you buy your ticket, on the internet?" and "Have you been on the high-speed train?" What he actually wants to know is what the hell a foreigner is doing on the cheap train.

6:59 PM

The ticket cost eighty-six yuan, about $12.50. The high-speed train would have been three times the price but only taken two hours, as it takes the most direct route.

7:12 PM

A passenger, male, mid-forties, strolls along the aisle, looks at me, stops, looks towards the window, then back at me, thinks things over, looks again and moves on.

7:22 PM

Train stops at Anshun, population 2.3 million. Never heard of it.

7:57 PM

A tubby gentleman in a suit and white shirt with polka dots sits opposite me and begins a conversation. The first sentence that I understand is: "You should find a Chinese wife."

7:58 PM

If my Chinese were better I would have answered: "The surplus of men in this country is somewhere around 40 million. Shouldn't you be a little more protectionist as far as your women are concerned?" Sadly, I don't know what the word for "protectionist" is in Chinese.

7:59 PM

The language barrier makes the conversation difficult, so I suggest using the translating function on WeChat. A Wi-Fi dead zone hinders this initially.

8:26 PM

Reception back, general relief. Polka-dot man types a message, and I use the translate function on my phone.

8:27 PM

The following message arrives on my screen: "Hello, I'm a red taurus from Thailand, glucose replenishment liquid chini. Welcome in China! Time have, to go to Henan to play? To my house?" The sender laughs warmly.

8:28 PM

He opens a briefcase and passes me two cans, one of Red Bull and one with "Energy Chinese Enhanced Energy Drink" on it. I now understand the first part of the message: he sells energy drinks.

8:30 PM

A cell phone photo is taken of two men: a drinks dealer with a wide grin on his face and a foreigner with a donated can. On the label: "Thaland Red Bullbeverace Company."

8:32 PM

It springs to my mind that the "play," which is *wan* in Chinese, from the message could be translated with erotic connotations. Will my trip end in a visit to Henan? Stay tuned.

8:35 PM

On the Energy Chinese Enhanced Energy Drink there is a picture of a famous actress. I joke that she is my Chinese girlfriend and trigger a fit of laughter lasting more than one minute among the listeners.

203

8:39 PM

An until then uninvolved listener slaps me on the shoulder and laughs. Party in car 17.

9:34 PM

The Red Bull dealer says good-bye with a handshake and a message that my cell translates as: "Man, keep your security on the streets." He then goes to the door with his briefcase.

9:36 PM

The train stops at Liupanshui, population almost 3 million. Never heard of it.

9:49 PM

Ticket inspection. The conductor looks at my ticket, then at me, then at my ticket, and then again at me.

10:11 PM

If a train compartment were a drum kit, then the snoring sounds would be the bass drum and the slapping of playing cards on the table the snare. I try to sleep.

12:13 AM

Stop at Xuanwei, population 1.3 million. Never heard of it. The car empties considerably. Only seven passengers holding out.

2:49 AM

The conductor walks down the aisle announcing, "Qujing, Qujing," which is the next stop, in a loud voice. Population 5.9 million. Never heard of it. Dammit, awake again.

4:03 AM

Soothing piano music is coming from the train's speakers. SOOTHING PIANO MUSIC! At four in the morning!

4:08 AM

Legal question: Can I sue pianist Richard Clayderman for bodily harm, even though it wasn't his decision to play "Ballade pour Adeline" three times in a row on a Chinese slow train?

4:33 AM

The train stops. "Kunming!" shouts the conductor. Too early, I think, as according to the schedule it should arrive at 5:05. Nonsense! I was mixing up arrival and departure times.

4:40 AM

Good news: the station here is not crowded at this time of day. Bad news: I'm suddenly being followed by a young man with a bundle of bills in his hand.

4:46 AM

If I speed up, he speeds up, too. When I slow down, he slows down. Always about ten feet behind me, even outside the station.

5:01 AM

Only by crossing to the other side of the street do I shake him off. I will never discover what he wanted from me. I get into a brand-new shuttle bus to the airport to fly to Baoshan. I'm back in the future.

THE MASTER'S VOICE

To: Bo
Morning! Just landed

From: Bo
Hello! Tell me when you are on the bus!

To: Bo
Er. Is it really 100 miles from the airport to Tengchong?

From: Bo
Which airport are you at?

To: Bo
Baoshan

From: Bo

BO FROM TENGCHONG could quite easily have told me at which airport I was supposed to land. His online profile says he lives in Baoshan, but on arrival I notice on the Tencent map that it is almost a hundred miles to the arranged meeting place, and that it apparently takes one day, fourteen hours and two minutes to get there. Big shock. Only then do I notice that the "on foot" setting is on. By car, it takes two hours and fifteen minutes.

In the course of further WeChat conversations, Bo proves to be pretty fond of telling me lots of things that don't really help me. Between a number of emojis crying tears of joy and cute animal GIFS, he explains that the nearest airport to Tengchong is called Tuofeng, A friend of his from Taiwan made the same mistake, and strangely enough, the Couchsurfing site automatically selected Baoshan as the region's name as the friend was trying to type in his home city. Incidentally, it is very easy to mix them up, as Tengchong is part of Baoshan.

After all that has been cleared up, Bo finally comes up with some information: I have to take a cab to the bus station, then a two-and-a-half-hour bus journey, and he will meet me at my destination.

· · · · · · · · · ·

BO LIVES IN a lovingly refurbished historical building, two stories, wooden walls painted light red and a little inner yard with a half-open kitchen. There are potted plants everywhere; I had almost forgotten the harmony of Far Eastern decorative elements.

"Before I moved here, I lived in Suzhou, but in a big city I can't be creative," Bo says. "Everyone's just chasing money, power and success."

The thirty-nine-year-old is wearing a slightly oversized orange North Face fleece jacket and glasses with rectangular frames. He has straight hair to his ears with the hint of a part. Bo speaks slowly, often embellishing a sentence gradually with details and minor adjustments until it contains the essence of his thoughts. The formulation of a statement like "Plenty of work has gone into the house, but I enjoy doing it. Still, it looks better in photos than in reality" can be drawn out to take a couple of minutes. At the end of a successfully completed thought, he usually laughs bashfully. Under normal circumstances, I would find a conversation with him somewhat lacking in appeal, but here, surrounded by so much haste and efficiency, Bo's long-winded and rambling but ingenious formulations are as beneficial as a retreat in a monastery.

He quit his job with an IT firm four years ago and now doesn't need a permanent office for his work translating patents and programming. He is a Buddhist and has discovered peace here that he missed elsewhere.

"There are a few problems, but the advantages outweigh them," he says, or that is the gist at least; he used ten times the number of words necessary.

When he first moved here three years ago, the landlord used to visit him every day. "He wanted to see whether I was a decent person, whether I was doing things right. 'You should leave the door open here and speak to the neighbors; otherwise, there will be whispering.' The people thought I was rich because I came from the big city. My life here is much less anonymous, and it takes a while to get used to that."

Strolling along the pleasantly skyscraper-less streets, I, too, feel not very anonymous. Much more often than usual I am greeted by passersby, schoolkids in their tracksuit uniforms and jade sellers. Jade is this city's most important economic asset, imported from Myanmar. The border is only a few miles away. Enormous stores present the green, shimmering treasures in glass display cabinets, the prices cheaper than in the rest of China: small brooches for around a thousand dollars, polished precious stone tabletops for thirty thousand. Tengchong feels like a small town, and with 600,000 inhabitants, by Chinese standards it is actually relatively small.

In front of a Vero Moda clothing store, a young woman in red linen pants, a gray linen blouse and a baseball cap approaches me. She wants to know where I come from, what I'm doing here and whether I'm interested in teaching English because, at the moment, they are looking for foreign teachers.

"I'm only here for two days," I tell her.

"Oh, that's too short," she says. "Can we still have a chat?"

"About what?"

"Some things. My name's Xiao Hu."

She gathers three plastic bags of clothing from her moped, then leads me to a lobby with an elevator and presses four, which has a "KTV" plaque right next to the button. A karaoke bar is not exactly a typical place for an innocent chat. I decide to be careful and prepare for a quick getaway.

We get out of the elevator and she guides me to a couple of seats not far from reception, where you can book karaoke rooms or tickets for the movie theater next door. We sit down and I ask Xiao Hu what she does in Tengchong.

"I am part of a group with a master who teaches us about Chinese culture." She speaks quickly, almost racing, as if the next sentence wants to overtake the previous one.

"A religious group?" I ask.

"Not totally, but there are elements of Buddhism, Christianity and the teachings of Confucius. Master is coming soon. It's his birthday today and he is celebrating a little."

There follows a monologue about how her life has improved since she met the "Master." Previously, she had often been ill, with bad skin and pimples that neither Chinese nor European medicine had helped. But things have improved greatly since she started following the Master's teachings. She believes that he has special powers and can sense other people's thoughts and emotions. "We live in a pretty house, and the training takes ten years."

Then, from around the corner, here he comes: the Master. He is a chubby little man in track pants, a T-shirt and leather sandals. His face glows as if he has been drinking. Xiao Hu gives him the plastic bags and he goes behind an empty counter at the other end of the room and proceeds to change.

"On your birthday you can get into KTV and the movies for free, and even get a complimentary foot massage. That's what he's doing today," she reveals.

He comes back dressed in linen clothes similar to hers. He asks me whether I am the new English teacher from Colombia, and Xiao Hu replies no for me. Then he tells me, in his hoarse, deep voice, that they have to be going now.

"Can I scan your WeChat number?" asks Xiao Hu. "Maybe we could see each other again."

I hold up the QR code on my cell, and then the Master and novice go on their way.

· · · · · · · · · ·

"OH, I KNOW the group," says Bo when I tell him of my encounter back at home. His inner courtyard is like an island of peace, hidden between side streets, two hundred yards from the main road. "They wanted to recruit me once. I had a talk with the Master, but he didn't really impress me." He pours two cups of Fujian tea. "I have met many religious men, and sometimes, in their presence, I have really sensed something. In Tibetan monasteries, for instance. He, however, spent most of the time talking about himself in that artificial deep voice. And he said I would find a woman quickly if I joined his group." He laughs shyly; Bo has had a girlfriend for years. But he can understand how the Master finds his followers. "China's greatest religion is money. Everything revolves around it, and that's just the way the government wants it. But many people feel that something's missing and they are searching for meaning."

The government in Beijing views beliefs of all varieties with mistrust, even if the main religions are no longer forbidden, as they were in Mao's times. People who are only interested in earning money don't start revolutions, whereas people pursuing ideas and wisdom are more likely to develop doubts about socialism. They fear parallel power structures that could challenge the state, which is why monks, priests and imams have to register with the government and acknowledge the government's policy of "Sinicization of Religions," which coerces various beliefs into toeing the party line. The Falun Gong sect was outlawed because the authorities feared subversive tendencies.

In practice, most Chinese people see spirituality pragmatically rather than dogmatically—a prayer to a Buddhist statue does just as little harm as a donation to a Taoist monastery, a small family altar to ancestors, a lucky amulet or advice from a roadside palm reader.

Bo believes in the power of tranquility: a minimum of furnishings, feng shui, clear-cut lines and withdrawal to the inner self. In the evening, he lights joss sticks and plays the guqin, a plucking instrument with seven silk strings that rests on a stand in front of the musician. The title of the piece is "The Still and Clear Fall Night," which consists of long drawn out sounds, plenty of pauses for breath and floating tones. Every played phase seems to be working towards the next pause. Proof of virtuosity lies not in playing quick tone sequences but in creating a greater impact through the timing of the pauses.

"In Chinese art, the emptiness of the various shades of white in a painting are just as important as the rest of the picture. They create space for the imagination," says Bo, as the last notes fade away and the room returns to silence.

· · · · · · · · · ·

THE NEXT DAY I meet Xiao Hu on a street corner with a propaganda poster of the Communist Party. "Civilization Warms a City" is written on it in Chinese, Burmese and English. A few yards away there is a Buddhist temple. State and religion—competing ideologies, vying for obedience.

Xiao Hu has an electric scooter with tiny wheels and a back seat that isn't even a foot above the road. I have to tuck my knees under my chin to be able to ride.

"This scooter is really too small for foreigners," she says, and zooms off.

The extra weight seems to be causing her problems, as she snakes along and at the intersection brakes more severely than necessary.

"I never learned how to ride this thing. You don't need a license for it," she explains. "I have no idea about the rules of the road."

As if to prove this, she cuts across the road and carries on riding in the left lane of oncoming traffic but without causing much of an outcry, as many people do the same here. We stop at a park with lots of greenery, fastidiously clean tarred pathways and political slogans on colorful wooden panels that resemble the instructions on fitness trails. The twelve core socialist values are written on red displays, always with two keywords paired together: "Patriotism" above "Engagement," "Prosperity" above "Democracy."

Xiao Hu tells me about her training with the Master. "For the first three months you just relax. You *learn* to relax, to have healthy sleep, not too much and not too little. I had sleeping disorders when I came to him," she says. Again, she speaks so fast, as if she has three or four thoughts on her mind at once and has trouble getting them across in the given time.

"Master gave me forty-eight hours of recordings of his voice," she continues. "I listened to his wisdom, and finally, I found peace of mind. His voice has great power. Even if you don't understand all of what he says, his voice can heal illnesses. It even works on animals. No snake or spider would ever come into my room when I was playing the recording."

The park is on a hill, and two joggers puff by. "No Smoking" signs hang from the lampposts and, right next to them, are poles with surveillance cameras and red-and-blue police lights. I wonder whether they blink as soon as someone lights up? In China, anything is possible.

But there is also something for the digital overseers to look forward to: "Twice a week, Master and I come here with a mic and a speaker and we sing karaoke together," says Xiao Hu. She never uses the definite article when mentioning the leader of the sect. "When I was new to the group, I spent almost every minute with Master. I couldn't be away from him without feeling unsettled. Only after a year did it get better." She feels privileged because she was accepted into the group. "He has taught thousands, but only thirteen followers are allowed to live with him here. A stroke of good fortune. Recently, I wrote a letter to UNESCO and recommended him for the Nobel Peace Prize. I haven't had a reply yet."

I ask if I can meet him and she sends him a text message.

We arrive at a Buddhist temple with a viewing terrace. She goes inside to pray, and I stay outside to look at the city.

Tengchong is surrounded by green hills with a lake in the middle. A couple miles to the north, a replica of it is being constructed, the Chinese logic being: two lakes means the potential for twice as many tourists, so why not? Many residents have been forced to move as their old lodgings had to make way for the bulldozers. In a couple of years, a new express railway line will be completed to bring even more tourists here, to the jade stores, the volcano parks, the hot springs, the traditional villages (a pretty one called Xia Qiluo and one that is, unfortunately, too touristy called Hechun) and the memorials to the Second Sino-Japanese War. In the city center there is a quaint Mao museum, with propaganda posters, Little Red Books in all shapes and sizes, and pictures of Marx and Engels on the wall. Mao, the great hater of religion, is still revered almost religiously in some areas, especially in rural districts, where many Chinese people still keep pictures of him as lucky charms.

"What makes the teachings of the Master so compelling?" I ask Xiao Hu.

215

"Unconditional love," she says. "Even when he is punishing you, you know that he loves you. You cry, but you feel safe with him."

"What kind of punishments?"

"You will find out for yourself when you come back and spend more time with us."

Xiao Hu's cell phone rings, and she speaks in an excited voice. Almost simultaneously, I receive a text message.

From: Bo
I just want to give you some advice: don't meet the Master.
I think the group is banned by the government and members are sent to prison.

To: Bo
I will be careful, thanks!

Xiao Hu ends her conversation. "Master says we can speak to him now. Coming?"

"Sure."

"We have to hurry. I'll leave the scooter here. Hopefully, we can find a cab quickly."

She types frantically into her Didi app and looks left and right with pursed lips. "Why is it taking so long?" she asks, jigging from one foot to the other, her eyes alternately on her app and on the street. After three minutes, a black cab pulls up for us. "*Kuai dian*—quick," she says to the driver.

A short while later, he stops in front of an entrance between two old buildings on the outskirts of the city, not far from the construction site for the new lake. Xiao Hu walks purposefully ahead through a door to a walled courtyard that would be perfectly suited as the backdrop for a Chinese historical movie: impeccable floor paving, weathered soapstone lion statues on the veranda, timbered walls with red lanterns at the doors and embellished grilles in front of the windows.

"Master found the property—8,600 square feet, fourteen rooms," says Xiao Hu proudly. "The building had been uninhabited for years. His intuition brought him here."

Well, the man has taste, I have to give him that. We sit down at a table near the entrance and wait. Xiao Hu tells me that in a few years everyone in the group wants to move on. They want to go to Tibet and Denmark first and later to Hawaii, to learn how to handle machine guns and helicopters. It is possible to do that there without complications, she tells me.

"You want to do *what*?"

"Oh, here he is."

The Master wears a white gown that resembles a doctor's coat, expensive-looking beige jogging pants and Adidas loafers.

"I've just come from a workshop," he says, and shakes my hand limply.

"What was the theme?" I ask.

"Everything. Many roads lead to Rome," he says, chuckling secretively.

The Master has a voice like syrup: ingratiating, deep, almost a whisper. It's a voice that sounds decades older than he looks, which is roughly in his early forties. I can imagine how such a voice could cast a spell on people. Xiao Hu brings a pot and pours us each a cup of jasmine tea.

"Do you like China?" he asks.

"Yes. I have found many friends, and I love the food. The developments over the last couple of years are stunning," I answer truthfully.

"Will you come again?"

"I hope so."

"Good. Tengchong is the best place in China."

"Why's that?"

"The area is full of beauty for the spirit. The clouds are different here. From these clouds you can detect that there is jade hidden in the hills. Once, we had a cloud above the lake that looked like an enormous phoenix. The air and the water here are special, and there are unusual rainbows. However, the construction sites are terrible, so we will soon move on."

From the corner of my eye I can see that Xiao Hu is hanging on his every word. She has probably heard these things dozens of times, but she still seems enchanted.

"Bring me my blade," says the Master, and she jumps to it.

Then, directed at me: "Do you like weapons?"

"Not particularly."

Xiao Hu returns and hands him a *guandao*, a kind of halberd, the jagged blade engraved with a dragon and the long pole made of rare wood. The Master turns the weapon lovingly in his hands. "Sometimes I play with it as if it were a friend," he says.

Xiao Hu elaborates: "Weapons also have a life. The longer they are with Master, the more powerful they become."

There follows a short discourse by the Master on the history of traditional Chinese thrusting weapons—contrary to the common belief, the *guandao* doesn't come from the third century Eastern Han dynasty times of General Guan, after which it is named, but the much later Song dynasty, in the thirteenth century. And, by the way, although it looks intimidating, it was better suited to training exercises than actual battle situations, in which a sword was much more practical.

While the Master speaks, he sometimes rests his treasure on his knee, turning it tenderly with his hand. When the blade is at the right angle, it catches the sunlight and illuminates his face.

I try to change the subject and ask what he teaches his novices. The Master asks Xiao Hu to explain. At supersonic speed, she gives a lecture about having to listen for the voice of the heart; about the right place in life; about quantum physics; about being surrounded by the tiniest of particles, and that these have to harmonize with heart particles; about finding peace and renouncing greed; about self-delusion and routine adjustments; and about one's own will that wrongly tries to control things instead of adapting to the realities of nature.

"One exercise was to write down everything I had done wrong up to then. I needed a lot of courage to do that, because accepting the truth can be painful. I cried for many nights. All negatives had to come out, had to come to light. Afterwards, you are a new, better person," Xiao Hu explains.

Her last sentence reminds me of the social credit system. Everything bad is made public and then people are better? Sounds like a wonderful utopia, but the question is: Who decides what is good and what is bad? And what if this person or institution is not really interested in the followers' enlightenment and well-being but simply pursuing their own interests?

"You can choose whether you want to live a free life or be a prisoner," says the Master in his deep voice. "Maybe you would like to come back again next year and spend more time with us. Think about it."

He stands up, leans his weapon against the wall and leaves the courtyard through a side door.

Xiao Hu beams at me. "You feel different now, don't you?"

"Hm, I'm not sure."

"Yes, you are. You're like a different person. Not so tired and bored like you were with me."

"He had a weapon."

"Very funny. Everyone changes with him. His mere presence heals."

. . . .

BACK IN THE city center I see an advertisement in a car dealership that depicts an Audi A8 as if it were a divine manifestation, surrounded by little stars with angel wings on both sides. Three buildings farther away is a gem store with a gigantic jade Buddha that, according to the price tag, costs the equivalent of US$550,000. What are the good people of Tengchong to believe in? Money? God? The party? The Master?

My acquaintances here have made their choices. Bo decided to escape the competition for riches and career, and found the old house, his instruments and Buddha.

Xiao Hu, striving for self-optimization, to defeat her inner demons, found the Master. Their two lives could hardly be more different, but both have left conventions behind and discovered a niche. Both, in their own way, are dropouts, who worship neither money nor the Communist Party.

At a further meeting with Xiao Hu I have to ask her why the group wants to take a machine gun workshop in Hawaii.

"Even Confucius advised practice with weapons," which then inspired the Master, is her somewhat vague answer.

Then she has another announcement to make: "We met on the fourth anniversary of the founding of the group, on Master's birthday. That is a sign," she says. "I know that you will come again."

I am no clairvoyant, but I think she's wrong.

220

HITCHHIKING
TO SHANGRI-LA

THE COMFORT OF a bus ride can be calculated from the parameters of length of journey, year of vehicle, number of fellow travelers, friendliness/size/manners/body odor of the person next to you, quality of upholstery, cleanliness and maintenance of vehicle, skill of driver, onboard entertainment, unexpected happenings, weather, view, ventilation system, food supplies, one's own orthopedic condition, behavior of other vehicles and the legroom/body length coefficient.

For the ten-hour journey to Lijiang I manage to catch a pretty old, pretty small Yutong bus, model zk6808hd9. Every seat is reserved, and next to me is a sullen young man who spends almost all his time taking in nourishment from chicken feet to sausages to spicy rice crackers to fruit candies. The associated plastic trash brings the netting on the back of the seat in front of him to the limits of its stretchability. The onboard entertainment consists of war films with mean

Japanese soldiers and cunning Chinese ones. The road is immaculate and the views sometimes spectacular—I would have loved to have had more time to stroll through this lush, hilly landscape and its villages, to visit the Three Pagodas of Dali and take a boat trip on Erhai Lake. The afternoon sun between the clouds creates a unique light effect, making buildings and cliffs and water all seem to glow from within. All the other comfort factors are mostly within the realm of average, so I reach Lijiang in the evening tired but without any lasting damage.

I have been very lucky here with my accommodation. My hostess, Lily, owns a little boutique hotel overlooking the historic old part of town and simply offers me one of her guest rooms with a king-size bed and a squeaky clean bathroom—how you can treasure such luxuries after weeks with little privacy. At last, I can close the door and have a bit of anonymity.

Lily is in her mid-forties and wears a leather jacket, expensive jeans and red suede shoes—the outfit of a successful businesswoman. She spent her early years in Nanyao, a village of the Nakhi ethnic minority, and today she works as a hotel manager and a sustainable tour operator.

"We have trained twenty-eight villagers as tour guides," she says proudly. Life in her childhood village has changed enormously in the meantime. "Today, only people over sixty wear the traditional outfits, so soon, nobody will be left to wear them." And she tells of a transformation that you can hear about wherever you are in the world, be it Siberia, Argentina or Minnesota, when economic change turns life around in rural regions. "It's good that people now have more money and get a better education. But something is missing in how we treat each other. Previously, there was more of a community spirit.

We exchanged goods and helped one another. Now, there's just rich and poor, and the gap has become greater."

. . . .

THE NEXT MORNING I get up early to go to Jade Spring Park and do something really Chinese—take a photo at a place where millions of people have already done so. The Five Arch Bridge, Moon Embracing Pavilion and Jade Dragon Snow Mountain, with a couple of weeping willows in the foreground, look like a tableau straight out of a calligraphy textbook.

Five Chinese Sayings That Explain the Country

1 Rather an idiot who works than a sage who sleeps.

2 It is better to stumble on new paths than to mark time on old ones.

3 Beating and scolding are the emblems of love.

4 All things have two sides.

5 A person who speaks the truth needs a fast horse.

Some forty photographers with expensive cameras are crouching with me on the banks of Black Dragon Pool trying to find the perfect angle. The brave ones climb a tree with a not particularly thick trunk that extends above the waters.

Beneath the plum trees in the park, a thirtysomething man is practicing tai chi moves with names like White Crane

Spreads Its Wings and Golden Chicken Stands on One Leg. Just a few yards away, a couple of seniors fire up a boom box to indulge in a bit of synchronized square dancing to the strains of "Ya ya ya coco jamboo, ya ya yeah." What a juxtaposition of the generations—the young man seeking inner contemplation with the aid of meditative exercises thousands of years old alongside the elderly finding entertainment in the simple dance floor beats of the nineties. But it's striking how close the crude and the poetic can be on an early morning in a Chinese park. I marvel at the tai chi master, who maintains his concentration and keeps to his own rhythms, never losing his balance, just like the snowy mountain and the bridges remain undeterred by the photographers and simply continue their sublime existence. The noise and hurly-burly of the human world don't seem to disturb them.

I sit on a bench for half an hour, observing the young man, the elegance of the slowness, the pausing moments as an art form, the demonstration of power through tenderness. The sight triggers something in me similar to Bo's guqin concert a couple of days previously: a feeling of deep melancholy, a foreboding that something here is about to be lost irretrievably. These meditative, tranquil aspects of Far Eastern tradition seem to have been ousted from day-to-day life. It is difficult to believe that this is a country in which poets once elevated inner contemplation to the highest ideal, such as, for example, Wang Wei in the eighth century in his work "The Bamboo Grove."

224

Sitting alone among dark bamboo,
Play: lift my voice, into deep trees.
Where am I? No one knows.
Only White Moon finds me here.[13]

And now? The next song blares from the stereo speakers: "Bang, bang, bang, catch me if you can. If you get me started, we could have a party tonight." Is China running away from itself? Has the country lost its gentle, calm side? Or should the young tai chi practitioner give us hope? I have often observed nowadays that it is the young who educate their elders, not vice versa, about having good manners or not leaving behind too much food at lunch, a bad habit that is still very common, for instance. On the cobblestone pathways in the old part of town, the usual massive jostle of tourists abounds, hordes of people crowding between renovated timber buildings in which you can buy hundreds of thousands of things; consumption and selfies and clamor rule, instead of simply letting your spirit flow. How absurd Western vacation ideals of rest and relaxation must sound to the modern Chinese, who just want to get the most enjoyment and excitement possible out of their few free days a year.

For me, there is no point in staying longer. I go back to the hotel, pack my bags and take a cab to the outskirts. I want to get away from the hustle and bustle, away from the cities. In the scorching heat, I wait at a roundabout and ask total strangers whether they can take me to Shangri-La.

North of here are the mountains and high plateaus of Yunnan and Sichuan, places that are so scantly populated that it would be impossible to find a Couchsurfing host. So, for a while, I will try to get to know the locals without the help of digital resources—for instance, by hitchhiking.

Only a tour bus stops in the first half hour, but it is heading for Kunming in the south. I approach an suv driver wearing a Hugo Boss sweater and a Swiss watch who pulled over in a bmw x1 to use his cell phone. He also wants to go to Kunming, but was planning to go back into town briefly for something to eat.

In the next half hour, precisely two cars stop, but both are going in the wrong direction. I find myself thinking a very Chinese thought—what a waste of time standing on a roadside instead of looking for a driver with my Didi app (unfortunately, I can't use the Didi app, as you need a Chinese bank account).

The SUV driver returns. "No car?" he asks.

"No car," I answer.

"Okay, I can take you to the first exit on the highway."

And then I'm sitting in the passenger seat of his luxury vehicle. He offers me a bottle of water and introduces himself as Jackie. As we pass through a tunnel, he points and says: "My job." He is an engineer and the boss of a tunnel-building company with a hundred employees. After ten minutes, he lets me out behind a toll station.

I'm back on the roadside, but at least this time all the traffic is heading in my direction. I ask myself what the officials at the toll station think about a pedestrian on the highway, but nobody bothers me.

Shangri-La is the name of the next sizeable town, 106 miles north of here. Since the British author James Hilton gave the name to a mystical utopian valley deep in the Tibetan mountains in his 1933 novel *Lost Horizon*, the term has caught on in the tourism industry. With no further ado, two places in Yunnan and Sichuan were so named, and in India, Bhutan and Nepal there are other Shangri-Las.

226   A white SUV passes me, brakes and then reverses. For a moment, I think Jackie has come back for me, but this car is a Dongfeng Fengguang, which is half the price of his BMW. Such mistakes can happen in copycat China.

I am greeted from the front seats by Selina and Calvin, forty-one and forty-two, a married couple on vacation. They both look as if they have just come from a fashion shoot: she in military jacket and frayed hot pants with dozens of different-colored braids in her hair, he in casual patched jeans and a shirt with "warrior" printed on it.

"Shangri-La? Sure! Did you wait for a long time?" asks Selina.

"Only five minutes. I'm so lucky you stopped for me!"

And then we are hurtling north accompanied by Chinese pop music. Selina and Calvin both come from Hangzhou and have a thirteen-year-old daughter who is staying there with her grandparents. They only have ten days of vacation a year and are quite happy to have some time to themselves for a change. He is part of a management team for a fashion company, and she has just changed jobs from running an English language school to working for a state-owned road construction company because "the conditions are better there."

From the windows, we can see Buddhist stupas and Tibetan lettering. Yaks graze at the roadside and the mountains are getting larger, many with snow-capped peaks; on one slope I can see the concrete piles of a construction site for the new express train.

We stop briefly at a scenic spot with a view of Tiger Leaping Gorge, a spectacular canyon through which the Jinsha River seethes like an unleashed elemental force.

Later, we stop at a roadside snack stand selling delicious dried yak meat in a chili marinade. Calvin takes the opportunity to buy two yak penises, which in traditional Chinese medicine are thought to be strong aphrodisiacs.

They drop me off in Shangri-La, where the name of the place is sadly completely misleading—it is a small dreary city, with a couple of Tibetan architectural elements and a huge shopping mall built in the style of a temple.

I stay the night in a simple hotel and try my hitchhiking luck again the next day early in the morning at the roadside. This time, I am less fortunate; in one hour, no one going towards Sichuan province stops. As there is only one bus a day, which leaves at 9:00 AM, I decide to take it rather than hope for the next white SUV.

Normally, the ticket office clerks would ask to see my ID card, but not here. It strikes me that I've now been traveling for quite a while almost incognito: staying in private accommodations, without the required registration with the police, and hitchhiking instead of buying a bus or train ticket. The last time I withdrew money was in Shanghai, and I don't use my cell to pay for things. If I switched off my phone with its Chinese SIM card, I'd be all but invisible—what a liberating thought.

Just a couple of hours later, I ask myself whether it might actually be better if somebody knew where I was. The dusty gravel road is barrier free on the valley side, where it goes steeply down into an abyss, and the bus driver must repeatedly drive around large boulders that have fallen from the cliff face.

We jolt over one pothole after the other, the straps and cords of a backpack in the luggage rack whipping against the cladding, a bottle rolling down the aisle at breakneck speed. It's impressive how the Chinese man in front of me is unaffected, despite the jolting and jerking, and manages to keep looking at the game he's playing on his cell phone. We are surrounded by nameless mountains higher than fifteen thousand feet. My head is thudding—I am feeling the first symptoms of altitude sickness.

People who want to know what this feels like should try out the following experiment: Fill a half-empty bottle of cheap rum with Coke. Drink it and then treat yourself to the cheapest red wine in a one-liter Tetra Pak from a discount store, followed by three shots of tequila without salt or lime. Strictly no accompanying food or water is to be taken before falling asleep. The next morning, pull on a rubber swim cap that is three sizes too small, pulling your face taut, and swig down three cups of iced coffee to get the pulse up and running. To simulate insufficient oxygen intake, put your hand over your mouth and nose and exhale so heavily that pressure is exerted on your eyeballs.

This is how my head feels while I watch four police officers who stopped us rummage through the luggage compartment and then walk through the bus. The youngest one takes photos of all the passengers. This bus trip deserves considerably less comfort points than the previous one, from Tengchong to Lijiang. The occasional mini-villages are now totally in Tibetan style, with cuboid whitewashed buildings with colorful trapezoid-shaped window frames. Chinese flags competing with Tibetan prayer flags flutter from the flat roofs; flying the

Tibetan flag is forbidden. It's a pity I'm not able to look inside these houses. How superficially we travel when we're not able to enter people's homes!

In the 1950s, the "peaceful liberation of Tibet," or China's takeover of Tibet, was undertaken with such military force that the Western countries described it as an annexation and the Dalai Lama had to flee to India. The region had previously been autonomous for decades. As so often happens in land disputes, the two sides are deeply divided, and you can find those who passionately believe Tibet should belong to China and those who believe just as strongly that it shouldn't—their main difference is which century they use as a historical reference. In the end, the winner is the one with the bigger army.

230   From the Chinese viewpoint, they rescued the poor Tibetans from a medieval feudal system and gave them the chance to improve infrastructure and gain prosperity. The many Han Chinese who work and do business in Tibet see themselves as

missionaries of economic progress that was only made possible by generous investment from Beijing (the Han are the largest ethnic group in China, with a population of more than 1.2 billion). From the Tibetan viewpoint, their mass immigration to Tibet is cultural imperialism, destroying their ancient traditions and bringing economic profits mainly to the Han.

· · · · · · · · · ·

I SPEND THE night in a dusty valley village named Xiangcheng before I move on by hitchhiking. An uncommunicative couple from Chengdu picks me up in a VW Golf without license plates but with plenty of luggage. We travel on an immaculately tarred serpentine road up to the pass at thirteen thousand feet, where black yaks graze on the mountain slopes and herdsmen's motorbikes lean against bare stone huts. On the high plateaus of Sichuan, drivers of small vehicles without four-wheel drive can reach heights that in the Alps are only reachable by skilled mountain climbers. My headache, thank goodness, is better than it was yesterday.

My destination is once again called Shangri-La. Until it was renamed a few years ago, the place was known as Riwa and is at the entrance to the Yading Nature Reserve. But here, too, the name doesn't seem to fit—huge parking areas for tour buses and one new hotel after another. James Hilton would turn in his grave if he knew what happened to his idea. By the way, he had never been to the high plains of Tibet; he read an article by the Austrian-American explorer Joseph Rock in *National Geographic*,[14] and then he just let his imagination run wild from his desk in the London suburb of Woodford.

My benefactors drop me off not far from a lavish entryway. In the booking hall I pay a sumptuous 270 yuan fee (forty U.S. dollars) for the national park and walk up a few steps to a brand-new shuttle bus with spotless seats that smell of fresh leather.

Just as the driver is about to close the doors, another passenger comes running up, a young man with thick glasses and pristine new trekking gear. Flustered and totally out of breath, he thanks the driver. After a fifty-minute ride through a spectacular mountain panorama, I get out at my destination, which is described on sichuantravelguide.com as follows: "Yading used to be a small village, but now it is more famous as a tourist site which is also honored as 'the last pure land on this blue star.'"[15] Translation: "In this place you will not feel lonely and you won't find a garbage dump." None of the gray stone buildings seems to be more than ten years old—everything was probably flattened and rebuilt, as usual, to afford visitors reasonable comfort.

I had already noticed this in the Tujia villages, but I will never understand the Chinese aversion to anything old, even if there are perfectly logical reasons for it. A sentence like: "Things used to be better in the olden days" doesn't suit the pragmatism of a people who had every trace of sentimentality purged by the Cultural Revolution. People in Europe think that structures built more than a hundred years ago are often of a higher quality and more stable than those built today. Many Chinese people think that old houses have catastrophic drainage systems and are freezing in winter. When they travel to Europe, they are often surprised by how old-fashioned everything is.

In my hotel, there are illustrations of tigers in the halls and Chinese flag stickers on the windows. I hear the sound of someone vomiting in a neighboring room. Sometimes in

China it is difficult to tell whether someone is throwing up or just spitting, but in this case, because of the volume and the sound of splattering, there can be no doubt. We are at an altitude of thirteen thousand feet, so these noises are probably not infrequent here, and I feel again a slight headache and a heaviness in my limbs that cause every movement to be at half the normal speed. Between the two beds is an oxygen unit with a mask and an emergency number to call before using it.

Shortly before ten, there is a knock at the door.

"Yes, *ni hao?*" I say.

A woman's voice answers in Chinese. I don't catch a single word.

It is advisable to behave defensively with lady visitors at night in Chinese hotels. Unless of course you want a "massage" with a few additional services that are not strictly necessary from an orthopedic standpoint.

Again, I hear the voice, this time the tone more urgent. I open the door. Standing in front of me is a small woman in a Tibetan *chuba*, a sheepskin coat, holding something that looks like a kind of blinking Tamagotchi. She asks for my index finger, which she clamps into her device. Ten seconds later, she releases my finger and looks at the display. An 88 and a 105 are shown, and she nods contentedly.

"*Hao bu hao*—everything okay?" I ask.

"*Hao*—good," she answers, giving me a thumbs-up. Considering the circumstances, I seem to be healthy. I later discover that the 88 is the percentage of oxygen saturation in my blood. A reading near 100 is normal, but in high mountain regions, 88 percent is fairly okay. And the 105 is my resting pulse rate, which is much higher than usual; apparently, my heart is having to work pretty hard to cope with the thin air.

233

The woman goes to the next room, and I return to my bed. It's a good thing that visitors are medically monitored because people staying at this altitude without acclimatization risk having life-threatening lung or brain edemas. I take a Tylenol for my headache and try to sleep.

GOD OF WISDOM

I WANTED TO GET far away from civilization, but the next day shows me once more the perfection of the Chinese tourist industry: again, a luxury shuttle bus (a young man, the same one as the day before, climbs aboard in the nick of time) takes me to the start of a short walk over stone steps and wooden walkways that ends in a parking lot. There await some twenty neon-green electronic minibuses that resemble golf carts. I climb into the first one with a couple of other tourists in brand-new outdoor gear and sneakers and, with a high-pitched screeching of the motor, we soon hurtle off on a narrow but immaculately tarred road through the undergrowth. The breakneck speed indicates that the driver isn't expecting any oncoming traffic. Our destination is the Luorong steppes, a network of wooden walkways over grassland plains. The landscape is still covered in morning mist, but I can just make out a couple of horses and some huts on the slopes.

I intend to be very careful about what my body is telling me and turn back immediately if I don't feel well, but

I would dearly love to get as far as the famous Milk Lake, which lies at an altitude of fourteen thousand feet. According to the guidebook, it's a three-hour slog to get there. I set off on the clean, smooth wooden planks. Mountain trekking in China is often a disappointment—at least if you're expecting to experience unspoiled nature. On previous travels, I have climbed some of the holy mountains of Taoism, such as Huangshan in Anhui province and Huashan, or Mount Hua, near Xi'an. Access to the peak in both cases is just a matter of trudging up steps and can be accomplished in loafers, and there are stands selling touristy keepsakes, souvenir photos and snacks every hundred yards. It's cardio training with noodle soup fumes, not a getting-away-from-it-all experience.

But here, I soon reach a path with no wooden walkway or railings. Occasionally, cheerful Tibetans pass by, some carrying buckets and tools for collecting trash. Then the mists lift and suddenly a white colossus towers above me: the north face of the 19,500-foot Jambeyang, a dream of a mountain with an almost perfect triangular peak, that Buddhists believe represents the god of wisdom. The explorer Joseph Rock described it in 1931 as "the most beautiful mountain I have ever laid my eyes on," and I can well understand why. In the novel inspired by Rock, Lost Horizon, the Shangri-La paradise can be found not far from a "perfect cone of snow" named Karakal. The description matches. Am I finally about to discover the real Shangri-La?

236   A white-eared pheasant with a red head and red feet waddles right across my path with no signs of shyness and disappears into the scrub between the conifers. A squirrel skitters up an oak, Himalayan blue sheep look down at me

inquisitively from a slope, and I am escorted by bumblebees and butterflies. It's all happening out here in nature.

Tibetan flags, a sign of human presence, flutter regularly from trees and cairns, particularly on a plateau from which I can see the other two giants: Chanadorje (19,547 feet), with its flattened, smooth snowy summit and what appears to be the profile of a face on its slopes, and Chenrezig (19,790 feet), with its steep trapezoid-shaped sides leading to a summit clump that also resembles a face. Like stage smoke, the clouds ascend the mountain face, a glistening network of snow and rock that resembles huge Sanskrit lettering. I am not at all surprised that this wonder of nature is revered as a bodhisattva, a divine being. At the side of the path in a rotting wooden frame hangs a single dented tin prayer wheel. It squeaks loudly, one squeak per turn, and somehow, that sound fits in with the ordeal of the ascent.

Soon I reach the blue-green, shimmering Milk Lake, a peaceful place surrounded by some of the most spectacular mountains in China, rocky symbols of the everlasting. They were here 100,000 years ago and looked just the same even then—a reassuring thought. There are only four other hikers here; the grazing Himalayan blue sheep are definitely in the majority—there must be hundreds of them. Their name, by the way, is misleading, they have brown fur and are more closely related to goats than sheep.

I sit down at the lakeside and munch a few digestive cookies. I only have half a package and one and a half liters of water with me; after all, I expect to be back in the valley in the afternoon.

A young man with black glasses, a denim shirt and ski poles approaches. I know him somehow.

"Hi, I'm Vic," he says.

"Hello, you're the one who is always late for the bus," I answer, and he laughs.

"Are you doing the whole *kora?*" he inquires. He means the pilgrims' path clockwise around Chenrezig, which usually takes two days. It's twenty miles over two passes and supposed to be mighty good for the karma.

"Is it not pretty high and quite a long way?"

"From here, only six hours. You seem to be pretty strong and quick."

The Chinese and their copious compliments—he already has me wrapped around his little finger.

"Okay, I'm coming with you." Maybe I should join one of those career workshops where participants learn to say no. However, I could always turn back after an hour if the altitude proves to be too much for me.

238   So off we go. With every step, we are moving away from Jambeyang, the mountain of wisdom, and getting closer to Chenrezig, which is considered the mountain of compassion. Vic is from Beijing, works for an IT company and enjoys

spending his vacations outdoors. His cell phone displays the route on a website that shows photos of key points. It shouldn't be possible to lose our way when all we actually have to do is keep the sacred mountain to our right. After an exhausting hour, we reach the highest point of the trail, a pass with a huge collection of prayer flags at fifteen thousand feet. The mountain panorama is as breathtaking as the ascent, and I am relieved that we will now be heading down to another lake.

I see two men with broad-rimmed cowboy hats crawling on the ground on all fours. One of the hats says, in big letters, "MADE IN CHINA," as if it's cool all of a sudden.

Are they particularly devout pilgrims? Way off.

"They are looking for *yartsa gunbu*, caterpillar fungus," explains Vic. "It's good medicine and costs up to three hundred yuan apiece."

His price estimate (around US$42) might be slightly too high, but *yartsa gunbu* really is one of the most expensive natural remedies in the world. In some regions of Tibet, it is the most important economic factor and has brought prosperity to whole villages. It develops when unfortunate butterfly caterpillars are eaten up from the inside by a parasitic fungus, leaving only the outer skin. When boiled in water, it is supposed to be good for the lungs, kidneys, circulation, heart and cholesterol levels. It is also thought to protect against cancer and increase potency. Scientists, however, dispute these miraculous effects, and even the Chinese Ministry of Health recently released a statement discouraging the consumption of caterpillar fungus.

239

"Have you tried it?" I ask Vic.

"Yeah, a couple of times," he says. "I really did feel stronger afterwards."

Maybe we should have bought some from the fungus collectors right away because the route is proving demanding. The sun is directly above us, the sparse vegetation beside the path offering no chance of shade. I am dizzy, and our destination is still far away. None of this is sensible after only a couple of days of acclimatization to the altitude.

I count my steps, over and over again, one to six, in German, English and Chinese—six more is always a manageable number. After four hours, we have to ascend again to the next pass, almost as high as the first. In this country of 1.4 billion incredible effort seems necessary to find solitude in a place without surveillance cameras, without cell phone reception, without smog and without people. If I could think clearly, I would realize that I have reached my own personal Shangri-La. But I have to concentrate on the route, the loose scree without safety rails and wooden planks, six paces and then another six, on and on. And I have to ignore my increasingly bad headache without even thinking about my meager supplies of water and cookies.

An eternity later, the compassionate Chenrezig gives us two English hikers: Paul and Rudi, resting on the dry grass, with sunburned faces. They spent the night in a tent to split the trip in two parts and are amazed at our forced march.

"In *one* day? We already asked ourselves whether there really were people crazy enough to attempt that."

Out of sheer enthusiasm, they give us some raspberry and banana energy gels containing, according to the label, 290 percent of the daily requirement of vitamin C. I treat myself to two; maybe I'll eat one less apple tomorrow.

The rest of the way is downhill and leads to an enchanting forest. The floor is as soft as velvet and completely covered by pine needles, as if someone had flattened out a thousand anthills. And then we're back onto the walkways with the tourists and the signs describing the attractions. This time, I am almost pleased about all the commotion because we really did manage the round trip within six and a half hours. I thank Vic for coming up with the insane idea. Because of our extreme exhaustion we forget to exchange WeChat details on parting.

I am not a religious person, but today I act like the Chinese: pragmatically. Before climbing into the luxury bus and going back to civilization, I lay the palms of my hands on my chest and bow towards Chenrezig, where the god of compassion keeps a watchful eye on irrational hikers.

. . . .

THE NEXT DAY, after traversing another three hours of spectacular mountain roads, and 10 million serpentine turns, I reach the highest airport in the world: Daocheng Yading Airport, at 14,472 feet above sea level.

From outside, the departure lounge looks like a gigantic   241
silver UFO with scales on its exterior; the architect probably thought it made sense, being so close to outer space. A man with a wheeled case comes towards me with a portable oxygen

tank—not a bad idea; he probably just landed on the Chengdu plane and began his trip twelve thousand feet lower down.

A small restaurant offers dried yak meat, popcorn and instant noodles, and three check-in desks are dealing with passengers. An escalator with a notice stating, "Please don't stay" (meaning "No loitering," but at this unhealthy altitude the tip is justifiable) leads to the first floor, where there are benches and massage chairs that can be activated via WeChat. Less commonplace is the Oxygen Bar: a simple room with yellow walls that looks like a doctor's waiting room. Four oxygen dispensers bubble away on the wall. I stay here a while, breathing the air that really does feel less thin. I'm a bit puzzled, however, as it smells like cigarette smoke—an inept interior designer placed the smoking room right next door.

Surprisingly, just a few passengers use this service. Outside the Oxygen Bar, I can see from the strained faces that many people are struggling with headaches, and as soon as I leave the room, I immediately feel the pressure in my forehead again. So the ensuing one-hour flight to Chengdu offers some relief, even though it is taking me to a megacity, the kind of place that I have intentionally avoided for almost two weeks.

CHENGDU
Population: 14.5 million
Province: Sichuan

CHILD SUPPORT

FINALLY, I AM once again in the lowlands. I breathe in greedily, which in a Chinese city is a big mistake. After a couple of minutes, my throat is already raw from the smog.

"I don't know what you're complaining about," says Huanhai, my thirty-one-year-old host. "In winter, the air gets *really* bad because all the mountains around act like walls."

Huanhai is wearing a deep red shirt, pale red shorts and leather sandals. He holds his nose a little too high, as if he doesn't want to see the world through his glasses. We meet at the Sanwayao subway station, and from there, he takes me to my accommodation. I have my own apartment, which he usually rents out through Airbnb, and he sleeps somewhere else.

The apartment, on the eighth floor of a high-rise, looks like something out of a home store catalogue, with details that tell me almost everything about the owner: full book shelves (intellectual), a number of vases with fresh flowers (aesthetic), cat Polaroids fixed to the fridge by panda magnets (fond of animals), five sofa cushions precisely equidistant (orderly to fastidious), exquisite tea service (pensive), designer bathroom with pretty tiles (clean), provocative photo of a male underwear model next to a wall clock (gay).

One year ago, Huanhai could no longer bear living in this apartment because he used to share it with Shen, his long-term boyfriend. Too many memories. He now lives with friends in a shared apartment. Shen moved to Guangzhou and they see each other once a month. He found a better job there as a construction engineer because soon they will need a lot of money—they dream of having kids.

"A child costs 1.5 million yuan, and we want two, one from each father, a boy and a girl. We want *dai yun*, not adoption—how do you say it? Oh yes, we are looking for a surrogate mother in the USA." He speaks softly, often searching for the right word in English. "Unfortunately, you can't do it in China, but there are agencies that offer a comprehensive package, including flights and all the paperwork."

He hopes that in three years they will have saved up enough money: US$215,000 per child. Shen graduated from Tsinghua University in Beijing, one of the best in the country, which is why he is now earning a decent salary. Huanhai, however, has just quit his job in management of a logistics company.

"I want to have more time for myself before we have children because I will be the one mostly in charge of their upbringing," he says. At the moment, he is reading lots of books and overseeing three Airbnb apartments in Chengdu. "Twenty-five to thirty bookings a month, and only five-star ratings in all categories," he says proudly.

We arrange to meet the next morning for a bicycle tour, and then he leaves me alone.

THE NEXT MORNING the doorbell rings. First, only two arms appear, holding out a bag with *baozi*, or bread-like dumplings, and a plastic bottle with cold strawberry milk tea.

"Breakfast," announces a cheerful Huanhai, after following the arms across the threshold.

A bicycle tour in China means, of course, Mobike or Ofo bike sharing programs. After a couple of subway stops, Huanhai uses his Ofo account to reserve two bikes with clammy handles and extension marks on the seat post that end at a height of six feet.

The Cutest Panda Videos on Screens at Chengdu Station

1 Panda mom gathers baby panda after climbing down a tree.

2 Zookeeper holds up baby panda with arms and legs spread-eagled.

3 Panda balancing bits of bamboo on its head.

4 Young panda plodding through grass.

5 Baby panda climbing to a fork in a tree.

You ring the bell by pushing a rotary switch on the left handlebar, so every Ofo beginner accidentally creates a bit of a racket because they think it's a gear lever.

Huanhai rides ahead. The print on his backpack reads: "A great bag—a great me," and somehow, it makes sense. In some

245

moments, he seems so sensitive that he needs encouragement from an item of luggage.

The first stop is his favorite place in the city—a teahouse in Bauhaus style with twittering birds in the garden. Hot drinks are accompanied by marzipan-like green tea candies in the shape of flowers.

The Chinese say: "Don't go to Chengdu too young; it will make you lazy." In fact, you do get the impression that the people walk slower here than in Shanghai or Beijing and don't seem to always be in a hurry.

"I like the city because it's more liberal than others," says Huanhai. "My friends here think it's okay that I'm gay and that I quit my job. My father, however, knows nothing about either. He wouldn't understand."

Huanhai's father is eighty, and his mother would have been seventy-six but died a couple of years ago. Seventy-six minus thirty-one equals forty-five—Huanhai is not their biological child. He doesn't know his real parents; he doesn't even know in which province he was born.

"*Fanzi.* What's it called in English? Oh, yes, child trafficking."

He says it so casually, as if it were one of a number of totally normal options for having a baby. It's quite a twist of fate that his adoptive parents once paid money for him, and now he, too, will pay lots of money for offspring.

"They bought me from baby kidnappers because they weren't able to have their own children. It was very common in my village," he explains.

Today, there are severe penalties for such transactions. Every year, hundreds of human traffickers are jailed. Huanhai's relationship with his adopted father, a farmer in the eastern province of Shandong, is more practical than affectionate. "We see each other once a year at the Spring Festival. We don't talk to each other much. I know that I'm important to him, but we never talk about what I actually want." Visiting his village is torture for Huanhai, because he is always being asked when he is finally going to bring his wife. "Then I just want to die," he says.

Until well into the eighteenth century, same-sex love was not a taboo in China, at least if you believe what was then being written. During Mao's time, however, homosexuals were persecuted and even executed, even though it was said that the great chairman was rather fond of young male attendants rubbing his back. *Quod licet Iovi*, etc. Only in 2001 was homosexuality removed from the list of mental illnesses.

Today, in the big cities there are Pride parades and gay clubs, but there is still a long path ahead to widespread social acceptance. Partners can be found online for so-called lavender

247

marriages to conceal your true sexual orientation from your family. You can also hire a fake girlfriend to present to your parents at the Spring Festival.

"That's not for me. I would have to make up too many lies," says Huanhai. "And what would I do if my father were to visit me in Chengdu? It really does get too complicated."

Shen, however, has told his parents that he prefers men. "They cried for five whole years, but now they have come to accept it. And now that they know we plan to have children, they are much more relaxed," says Huanhai.

After a tour through a huge flower market—his second-favorite place—Huanhai asks a question that can get you in serious trouble in China: "Do you eat everything?"

"Yes," I answer.

"Even spicy?"

Again, yes.

So we ride to a restaurant where the speciality is called ji za, a spicy stew of chicken intestines floating in soup. It doesn't taste bad at all, but the fiasco comes at the end of the meal. You could compare it to a soccer game in which the goalkeeper has saved every close goal for a full eighty-eight minutes, with no signs of uncertainty, no mistakes, and then misjudges a simple fluffed shot that somehow bobbles through his legs and into the goal, and all the previous heroics are forgotten.

My fluffed shot is a red chili, none of which I had previously missed; they remained either in the pot or on the plate and didn't get anywhere near my mouth. But I am not paying attention for one second, and catastrophe happens. I sweat and start to cry.

"I think it was a bit too spicy for you," says my considerate companion.

The next stage of my Tour de Chengdu passes through a park next to the New Century Global Center, which is the world's largest building in terms of floor space. It is 330 feet tall and has a surface area of 18 million square feet.

I was here four years earlier and at that time the building marked the southern edges of the city. Now it is surrounded by various tall finished high-rises, and towards the south there are sixteen new subway stations. Recently, the local government announced that they were moving all their offices to the south, probably simply to signal the transformation—there had previously been only wasteland there. Next year they are opening two new subway lines, and Chengdu is hoping to apply for the Summer Olympics soon. China's laziest city? No way!

Huanhai thinks the city has also changed socially. "Many people in my age bracket have gay or lesbian friends in their social circle and find out that we are just normal people with normal problems," he says, on our return to the apartment. This is already progress compared to earlier times, when there was no chance of finding reliable firsthand information about the lived experiences of LGBTQ people. "As a kid in a farming community, I seriously believed that I was the only man in all of China who was into guys," says Huanhai.

NEW BORDER

O N THE PLANE I read a kind of love story from the Qing dynasty. When Chinese troops conquered the city of Kashgar in 1758, they took a Muslim woman called Iparhan back to Peking, where she became known as the Fragrant Concubine. She was famous for the beguiling aroma that enveloped her, even without perfume. Cloaked in silk and in a sedan chair, she was brought to the capital to be the emperor's concubine.

Then something happened, and there are different versions depending on who is telling the story. The Han Chinese say that she was given the most beautiful chambers and even an oasis with a date palm in the Forbidden City and, eventually, thanks to all the splendor, fell for the emperor. Thus, she became a symbol for the unification of Xinjiang with the rest of the empire.

The Uyghur version of the story goes like this: When she arrived in the Forbidden City, the sweet-smelling woman became terribly depressed. Although in the imperial court it was considered a great honor if the emperor made sexual advances towards you, she gauged the situation differently. She even hid a dagger in her sleeve as defense against the emperor's hated attentions. In the end, the emperor's mother suggested she either accept her fate or kill herself. She chose the latter to keep her honor intact.

This episode in the eighteenth century proves that there has been a strained relationship between Xinjiang and Beijing for a long time. The Uyghurs, the ethnic group native to the Xinjiang region, are a Turkic people with their own language and script, and many of them would like to be independent of China. This has led to fierce conflicts, and in the past fifteen years, hundreds of Han Chinese have been killed in riots and terrorist attacks by Uyghur nationalists. Beijing reacted with a ruthless campaign of surveillance and set up "reeducation" camps for those Uyghur people who appeared "too Muslim."

Xinjiang means "new border," and nowhere else in the country are the nefarious effects of extreme surveillance more evident.

Let's start with the holiest place in the province, the Fragrant Concubine's grave in Kashgar, and then work our way towards the mundane. Her sarcophagus is in the Afaq Khoja Mausoleum, the tomb of an old ruling family that is now an important pilgrimage site. People who come here are reminded that a Chinese emperor kidnapped an upper-class woman from Xinjiang to turn her into his courtesan in a move that was anything but sensible diplomacy. The mausoleum has a square base, four towers and a large cupola in the middle. Metal spires reach up to the heavens, but it looks like they have been trimmed; if half-moons once rested there, they were later cut off. Green-and-blue decorative tiles, a number of which are missing, girdle the facade. The building looks its

251

age; at long last, what I see before me is not a highly polished reproduction but the genuine past. It's a bit *One Thousand and One Nights*, a bit Silk Road romanticism. Even the obligatory garlands of high-tech cameras are attached to rotten-looking wooden posts.

Inside the mausoleum is a stone gallery embedded with some twenty-five sarcophagi. The names on them sound as if they come from another country: Shah Bikem Pasha, Apakhhan Azem Pasha, Turdi Hojam, Borhandin Hojam. Kashgar is China's westernmost city; the distance to Tashkent, Kabul or Islamabad is considerably less than to Beijing or Shanghai.

The tomb marked "Iparhan" is hardly visible, far back on the right in the third row, draped with an orange silk cloth with a red flower attached. There is much debate about whether the tomb really contains the mortal remains of the Fragrant Concubine. According to legend, after a three-year honorary procession traversing the country, her body was brought back to Kashgar. Many historians assume she was simply buried in Peking.

Centuries after the death of Iparhan, Xinjiang is still a region about which diverse tales circulate, depending on to whom you are speaking. Having said that, in Xinjiang it is almost impossible to ask the Uyghurs themselves. All contact with foreigners arouses suspicion. The fear of being sent to a "reeducation" camp forces the people to be extremely cautious.

So I arrive with very low expectations of having open discussions. I won't be spending the night with local hosts and won't be pushing people to talk to me. Also, just to be safe, I have deleted my Facebook and Twitter apps because the authorities sometimes check to see what people have on their cell phones.

In the cab from the mausoleum to downtown there is a small monitor next to the rearview mirror from which, at first, solemn choir and string music is audible and a Chinese flag can be seen fluttering in the wind. Then comes a video of a Mandarin language course in a classroom. A teacher stands in front of a blackboard and adult students repeat in unison the sentence she has written on the board: "Zhi shi wo de pengyou, renshi ni wo hen gaoxing"—"That is my friend, I am very pleased to meet you." The cab driver is probably not learning the language because he wants to but out of fear of landing in a camp if he doesn't.

In the old part of town, I meet Mei Li at a kebab restaurant. The "old" part of town is a bit misleading because everything here has been newly constructed: row upon row of three-story concrete houses with sand-colored plaster facades made to imitate the look of old clay buildings. The numerous police stations are also housed in traditional-looking buildings. A number of mosque doors are sealed with padlocks, many places of worship closed. Instead, lots of walls are decorated with panels of quotations from the Kutadgu Bilig, an anthology of aphorisms from an eighth-century sage. The quotes that have been chosen sound like Chinese propaganda—most of them are about staying on the straight and narrow and avoiding bad people. Visitors to the old town have to pass checkpoints, and Uyghurs have to show their passports.

I contacted Mei Li through the Couchsurfing website. She is twenty-six and Han Chinese but born and brought up in Xinjiang. She spent a year studying in Shanghai but, one after the other, her relatives called her begging her to return. She gave in to the family pressure and now works as an elementary school teacher. When she talks about the Uyghurs, it sounds as though she is talking about naughty children; maybe it has something to do with her profession.

"They are stubborn, always causing trouble," says Mei Li. "And it's difficult to communicate with them."

"Why?"

"No education. Most of them quit school after junior high, and then get simple jobs—street cleaners, bus drivers or security guards—because they don't like learning."

"You have no Uyghur colleagues at school?"

"Yes, we do. I was on vacation in Malaysia with one of them. On our return, she was questioned by the police. They wanted to put her in a camp. When she said she works as a teacher, she was spared. But they arrested her uncle just because he was in Saudi Arabia a couple of years ago, in that big temple for Muslims."

"You mean Mecca?"

254

"Yes, exactly, Mecca."

It doesn't take much to be a suspect in Xinjiang. People have been arrested just because the clock in their living room wasn't set to Beijing time but two hours earlier, the unofficial time in Xinjiang.

"They check all cell phones. If you chat with someone about questions of Islamic faith or use a prayer app, then you are sent to a camp," Mei Li says.

"And how long do people normally have to stay there?"

"Nobody knows. Many months. Only people who pass a test can leave."

"What kind of test?"

"I don't know. Nobody knows."

"Are you also careful when you use your cell phone?"

"When my friends in Shanghai call I never say anything negative about the situation here. I always write: 'Everything is fine.' They don't know what really happens in Xinjiang."

Mei Li then tells me about a new government project titled "United as a Family" that organizes visits by Han Chinese to Uyghurs. "The government calls us relatives. If you don't get along well with your host, you can just call the police and they take them away to a camp."

What a corruption of the idea of cultural exchange and hospitality—with state approval, propagandists and potential informers come to your own home. The people are sure to have a great time together.

An elderly local with a *doppa* cap and an illegal long beard ("abnormal beards" are against the law in Xinjiang, as are head-scarves for women) saunters by our table and stops to ask Mei Li where I'm from.

255

"Ah, German! Fascists!" he shouts, and wanders off.

My conversation partner feels that her opinions have just been validated. "You see! They know nothing. It's best never to speak to them."

"You just told me you were on vacation with a Uyghur colleague in Malaysia."

Mei Li laughs. "That's different. She is super!"

. . . .

IN TWO LINES, sixteen policemen dressed completely in black march through the pedestrian zone. This is the evening patrol between pomegranate sellers and kebab grills. They are all wearing helmets and have shields; some of them have machine guns.

Today is June 4, the anniversary of the Tiananmen massacre, and when a little girl on a red tricycle pedals towards the patrol, I can't help but think of the iconic photo from that time—of a protester standing alone in the path of a row of tanks. Here, coincidence has created a kind of homage, an instant in which a child in a floral dress and the two armed soldiers in the front row are directly face-to-face. The group of police slows slightly and the child pedals unhurriedly past them with her head held high, without taking her eyes off the men in black, as if she were trying to memorize their faces. The tricycle passes less than a couple of feet from the heavy boots; nobody else dares to come as close. Will the little girl remember this day later, or are such encounters simply routine in a city that feels like a war zone?

In the faces all around I can read fear, which is only natural when confronted by the serious faces of the young policemen, some with Han features and some Uyghur. The local population are deliberately recruited for the security forces with the goal of making China seem like less of an occupying power while at the same time guiding young people away from religion and towards patriotism. The slogan "A son in the army means prosperity for the whole family" can be seen on a recruiting poster on the main road.

As the patrol halts at a checkpoint to guard all cardinal points, another interesting image is created. Directly in front of them is a metal sign with a smiling cartoon figure depicting a policeman as "Officer Friendly." The grim reality right next to it transforms the illustration into a caricature.

Kashgar is a high-security zone, with metal detectors in front of every restaurant, shopping center and hotel, police stations and police cars on every corner, an enormous Mao statue in the center and the national flag in almost every doorway (people who don't display it are likely to run into trouble). Should the Chinese presence in Xinjiang be viewed as an occupation or a defense against terrorism? Or a mixture of the two? Whatever is the correct answer, the situation in Xinjiang reveals Chinas capability for ruthlessness. The Uyghurs have no choice—either they abandon their culture or face the fury of state authority.

. . . .

HORROR AND BEAUTY are often found close together, particularly in Xinjiang. For the first and only time on this trip, I book a tour: two days along the Karakoram Highway with an overnight stay at Tashkurgan, not far from the Pakistan border. With me in the minibus are a couple from the U.S. who work in Chengdu, three Chinese women and another German. The driver is from Hunan province and came here years ago as a soldier but switched to the less dangerous field of tourism.

257

Five of the Author's Favorite Places in China

1 The artist village of Dafen, Shenzhen. Here you can buy inexpensive yet perfect hand-painted reproductions of van Goghs and the *Mona Lisa*, or a portrait oil painting for less than thirty dollars.

2 The plank walk on Huashan, near Xi'an. The ascent up the mountain includes sections where the daring can discover whether they suffer from vertigo.

3 The Great Wall, near Chenjiapu. This is an unrestored section that is only ninety minutes from Beijing. Getting there is tricky, but you can find information at greatwallfresh.com.

4 Tagong. This small Tibetan town in Sichuan has plenty of hiking options for visiting the temples on the steppes.

5 Huaxi. China's richest village is seventy-five miles west of Shanghai. People who like quirky places should spend a couple of nights at the central luxury hotel in a 1,076-foot-high skyscraper in the middle of the village.

At a checkpoint on the outskirts of the city we are sent back; the rules have recently changed and foreigners must be registered at a different exit, where we are summoned to a building with eight parallel security scanners. We have to place our passports on a scanner, and then press our thumb on a fingerprint sensor while looking into a camera. The technology works with Chinese passports but fails with mine, even though I try several times. So at one of the counters a heavily armed security official scans our documents by hand and asks about our jobs and what we are planning to do on our trip. I keep quiet about my journalist activities, saying that I'm a teacher, which isn't a complete lie, since I've visited so many schools. Eventually, we are allowed to continue.

Half an hour later, we come to another checkpoint, where again the technology fails and the same procedure follows. Next to me, an Uyghur woman is being frisked thoroughly, and an official connects a cable to her cell phone presumably to check her apps, chats and contacts. If they searched mine, they would find the *New York Times* app, Wikipedia, VPN programs, and Iranian and Turkish contacts. If I were Uyghur, I would be in a camp tomorrow. It's a pretty bad feeling, seeing the woman sitting there and, for a moment, being glad I'm not Uyghur.

As our journey continues, the mountains get bigger, some of the rock faces shimmering red in the sunlight, and the villages get smaller. At the roadside we see, one after the other, yaks, sheep and camels. All of a sudden, the snow-capped peak of Kongur Tagh, the highest mountain in the Pamir range at 25,095 feet, emerges from the mist. We are at an altitude of roughly 10,000 feet, and I can hardly believe the height. The summit, above steep slopes, seems considerably closer and deceives the senses, probably because of the perspective, because we are so near to it.

How far can I trust my perceptions? To what extent is my trip an accurate reflection of today's China? How many facets have I left out? Which encounters revealed deeper truths? And which judgments can I allow myself?

Naturally, the people I met don't represent a complete cross section of Chinese society—through couchsurfing, I meet up with neither the richest nor the poorest people but mostly the middle class ones who are cosmopolitan and exceptionally hospitable. But far, far more is hidden behind what I can discover in a few months. For a comprehensive trip to China you'd be better off taking three years than three months, but then again, things change so quickly here that many insights from the first years would no longer be applicable by the end. Despite all the miles I've traveled on trains and planes, I still feel like I've gotten just a few glimpses into this complex society. Even so, a picture has emerged, something as visible as the giant mountain in front of me, even though the dimensions might not always be correct.

We round the next corner and the summit already disappears for the rest of the day. In its place is the massive Muztagh Ata, another giant, of 24,636 feet, that occupies the whole horizon. The outline of the summit is so rounded and broad that only with great difficulty can you see the actual highest point with the naked eye. There is a huge diagonal channel etched onto the mountain, as if it ruptured many thousands of years ago.

Directly below the mountain is Karakul Lake, where our driver stops for a short break. Soldiers are pitching a couple of tents on the lakeshore and indicate that we are not to take photos, but why on earth do they have to set up camp here, directly in front of this fantastic panorama? The souvenir sellers are friendlier, offering jade jewelry, white felt hats and fennel tea from their yurts. We don't buy anything and travel on.

The spectacle gets even grander at the Tagharma viewing deck, a platform that really deserves its name—a river snakes through the green plain, a few yaks graze on the lakeshore and on the horizon sits the jagged outline of the mountain range, looking like the teeth of a predator, repellent and dangerous and magnificent.

From now on, we could stop at each bend in the road—the landscape is simply that spectacular. At a few places, we can spot the ruins of old forts and mausoleums. I feel insignificantly small in this raw alternative to the bamboo groves and idyllic pagodas of ancient Chinese landscape art.

We spend the night in Tashkurgan, a dusty outpost whose name means "stone tower" in Turkic languages. From here, it is another eighty miles to the Pakistan border, and to the southwest we can almost see into Tajikistan and Afghanistan. The name of the cozy hostel is K2, as it is also not far from the second-highest mountain in the world.

Quiz question: How many of the fourteen highest mountains in the world are partly on Chinese territory? The answer is nine, which is more than in any other country. It's funny somehow that we don't associate China with high mountains, but then, there are other topics that sideline geographical superlatives.

The next day we drive back to the grim reality of racial profiling, checkpoints and "reeducation" camps.

· · · · · · · · ·

WHAT IS KNOWN about the massive project that aims to make dutiful Chinese citizens out of supposedly dangerous Muslims? A few years ago I had a discussion with a university professor in Beijing who said, "China is not stupid enough to maltreat believers in Islam. After all, we do business with Islamic states throughout the world. How would that look?" Now, it actually looks like the worst form of racial profiling, but the outcry, even in Islamic countries, is rather mild. There are important business ties with China, after all.

For a long time, Beijing denied running "reeducation" camps in Xinjiang, but at the same time, it was advertising for workers to build the camps and for supervisors with job experience in the penal system. Then, slowly, eyewitness reports began to trickle out that presented an increasingly clear picture of what was going on. Roughly 1 million of the 10 million Uyghur population have already been interned, and according to information from the United Nations, it could be considerably more. After satellite images provided pretty convincing evidence, China eventually owned up to running "vocational skills centers," where Uyghurs were provided with "free training."

Since 2016, Chen Quanguo is the provincial governor of Xinjiang. Before that, he was responsible for law and order in Tibet. An out-and-out hard-liner with vast expertise in establishing a police state, he was the perfect person to take over the proclaimed Strike Hard Campaign Against Violent Terrorism that started in 2014. He made things happen, as shown by the economic data: in 2017, expenditures on security technology in Xinjiang almost doubled compared to the previous year—up to 58 billion yuan, or US$8.2 billion.

Reports by Human Rights Watch concluded that the number of human rights abuses in Xinjiang is greater than at any time since the Cultural Revolution. They also claimed that there are severe limitations on freedom of expression, rights of privacy, religious expression and the right to a fair trial. In the camps, there are unexplained deaths and suicide attempts, and obligatory lessons in civics and languages. Internees are forced to sing songs wishing Xi Jinping a life of ten thousand years, and they have to learn rules, rules specifically for Uyghurs in Xinjiang—for example, they must say *ni hao*, not *salaam alaikum*, because no Uyghur language is to be spoken in public, and they must support the Communist Party.

Orders like that remind me a bit of Yangwei, the young car dealer in Foshan, and his Rules for Sales Staff. But the difference is that the consequences for not following the rules in Xinjiang are deadly serious. People who don't study diligently are beaten and have to remain in the camps longer. The *New York Times* came to the conclusion that Xinjiang is a police state that resembles North Korea, with a kind of formalized racism similar to apartheid South Africa.[16]

The Human Rights Watch report contains a telling sentence: "China's global influence has largely spared it from public criticism."[17] The country has considerably more leeway than ten years ago, and the limits continue to be tested.

ÜRÜMQI
Population: 3.5 million
Province: Xinjiang

FORTY PERCENT

ALIM, WHO LIVES in the capital city of Ürümqi, knows from experience what it is like to be watched constantly. First, because he is Uyghur and, second, because he works for the government, in the "social security" department that monitors citizens to establish whether they are dangers to public order. This department decides who is sentenced to "studying" in a "reeducation" camp.

Alim is not his real name, and I will not describe him or how I got to know him. He is taking a great risk just meeting me. I am not quite sure what prompted him to do so, as he is critical of many developments in his province but is not a dissident. To an outside observer, our conversation would look like a chat between friends, but I think we are both a bit skeptical of the other.

With cardamom tea, cucumber salad and a hookah pipe, we sit in a booth in a restaurant with opulent carpet and rare wood interior, more in the style of Baghdad or Beirut than China. Occasionally, the waiter replaces the coal in the hookah, but we don't appear to have any other witnesses. To begin, I tell Alim a bit about my travels, and he speaks about the difficulty of starting a business in Xinjiang. I guide the conversation towards his job and ask how he and his colleagues decide who has to go to a camp.

"The government can't look into people's minds, but there are certain red lines. If you touch them or cross them, then you will be sent to a camp, just to be sure."

"But isn't the government sometimes a bit too rigorous in doing so?"

"Sadly, that's true. The mother of a friend was sent to a camp because she visited her daughter who lives in Turkey."

"Even though she could prove that her daughter lived there?"

"It didn't make any difference—it's a Muslim country. If you look for information on foreign websites, you are sent to a camp. If you use Facebook or Twitter, you are sent to a camp. Also, if you take drugs or don't pay tax. This only applies to Uyghurs, of course."

Alim has a strong voice that radiates authority and pride—and resentment. I begin to suspect that one of the reasons that he is willing to speak to me is because he believes that nobody in the world should be able to stipulate who he is, and isn't, allowed to meet.

"Are the people in the camps allowed to contact their families?"

"Nobody can visit you there. But recently, the rules were relaxed a bit, and now one telephone call a month to family is allowed. Yesterday, I was on the late shift and had to visit relatives of people in the camps."

"That must be an unpleasant job."

"I would love to quit tomorrow, because it is so sad. People cry the whole time. I try to tell them that everything will be okay, but of course, I don't know if it's true."

He inhales the apple-flavored tobacco deeply, exhales a thick cloud of smoke and coughs. What an absurd job. But as long as he works for the system, he can feel safe. At the same time, people who work for the government have to abide by even stricter rules than regular citizens as far as religion is concerned. He could be fired if he is caught in a mosque even once.

"How do you explain the harsh government crackdown to those families?"

"Things have to move forward. Security and stability are important, and the Belt and Road initiative passes through Xinjiang. There can be no terrorism."

"How many Uyghurs are in the camps?"

"Forty."

"Forty?"

"Forty percent. You can't imagine how many camps there are."

Alim names an immense number. That would mean roughly 4 million people in prison, considerably more than the estimates by the UN or Human Rights Watch. Does he have better information? Or is he naming a target figure? Some reports say that 40 percent is the projected quota, but that doesn't mean the government has reached it already.

I ask him how he, as an Uyghur person, feels about doing such a job.

"I'm somewhere in the middle," says Alim. "I wouldn't side with the Uyghurs or the government. There was a problem with extremism, and we had to do something about it. And we were never independent as a state. Now we belong to China, and we'd better accept it."

But that is exactly what many people find difficult, particularly as for many decades, the Uyghurs have felt forcibly sidelined economically and culturally by the mass immigration of Han Chinese. In 2009, there was a mass brawl at a toy factory in Shaoguan in Guangdong province between Uyghur and Han Chinese workers in which at least two Uyghurs were killed.

As a result of the Shaoguan incident, a demonstration was held in Ürümqi. According to Alim, the mood was inflamed by a video that was doing the rounds on social media. The video shows a murder: an Uyghur-looking girl dances on the street and a man gets out of a car and attacks her, stoning her to death. The video went viral as apparent proof of how the Han Chinese treat the Uyghurs. As shocking as the deed was, however, it had nothing to do with China. In fact, the video was already a couple of years old and came from Uzbekistan, but what power do mere facts have when the content is so emotionally charged?

"I was astonished. Even seriously intelligent friends of mine, people with university degrees, weren't questioning what they were seeing. They got very angry about the Han Chinese."

The authorities sent the military to the demonstration on July 5, 2009. There were hefty clashes, and a mob with clubs and knives took to the streets searching for Han Chinese. By evening, more than 190 people were dead. Further attacks followed; for example, in Kunming in 2014, when Uyghur rioters killed thirty-one people. Now, anti-terror measures have become a pretext for the state to enforce the assimilation of a whole ethnic group.

267

Alim says the situation has gotten really out of hand since the hard-liner Chen Quanguo came to power. "He is completely crazy. Seriously, I hate him. He doesn't give a damn about people. He says, 'Okay, if you want a fight, we'll give you one.' He was the one who decided to set up the camps. And there are a couple of other local governors, in Kashgar and Hotan, for instance, who use their power simply to send everyone they don't like to 'study.' The people are incredibly scared."

· · · · · · · · · ·

EVERY TIME I go back to my downtown hotel, the security gate beeps, triggered by my camera, cell phone and wallet. Nevertheless, the tired guard waves me through to the elevator. I don't have to place my ID card on the scanner that then shows all the important information about a person on an iPad-sized screen, because I have a foreign passport that doesn't respond to this system, and because I don't look like Uyghur. A black riot police protective shield with a bulletproof viewing window leans on the wall next to the guard. You see these shields everywhere in Xinjiang: symbols of a province in a constant state of readiness.

And everywhere you look, the red-and-blue police lights blink. At no point on any street in the city center can you do a 360-degree turn without seeing at least one police post, or a police car with tinted windows. The regulations for downtown are: one police post every three hundred yards.

During my tour, I am stopped twice. First, by a polite policeman on the roadside who wants to see my passport. Then, while taking a snap on my cell of the large mosque near the bazaar, I have a less friendly encounter.

A young man in uniform blocks my way and another climbs out of a car and asks: "What's the problem?"

I am asking myself the exact same question when he speaks into his walkie-talkie. We are joined by a third policeman who appears to be their superior. All three are equipped with heavy machine guns.

"Delete," the boss says. "No photos of the mosque."

"Why not?" I ask.

He just says: "Bazaar photo okay, mosque no."

After deleting the photo in front of him and showing my passport again, I am allowed to continue.

On the way to the bazaar forecourt, I pass more metal detector gates. They are made by a company called Guard Spirit, and on one of them is written: "Please accept inspection consciously." The local population puts up with the checks with a kind of stubborn resignation.

Then I am in an inner courtyard with an immaculately renovated tower and brick buildings. At the moment, there is a dance performance in traditional costumes with the musical accompaniment of three drummers and a trumpeter on a roof directly beneath a Chinese flag.

Tourists form a circle around the graceful dancers in their colorful brocade clothing and take photos, some swaying to

269

the music. Later, they stroll through the endless alleyways of the bazaar, marveling at the clothes, the delicacies and the handicrafts. The setting is almost a bit too clichéd, a perfect multicultural world, smelling of patchouli, myrtle, and leather, on a sunny day right in the heart of Ürümqi. Daggers are also on offer in the bazaar, but Uyghurs are not allowed to buy them, though traditionally, fathers presented their sons with decorative daggers on their eighteenth birthdays. Nowadays, the state even monitors how many kitchen knives a Uyghur family owns.

I take a cab to Hongshan Park. It is very green, very family friendly, and as secure as a prison. The name translates to "red mountain," because the park is located on top of huge reddish rock formation that used to be bleak and craggy until, in the 1950s, the Communist Party and many volunteers planted thousands of trees to make it more appealing. Today, the greenery is protected by fences topped with razor wire and heavily guarded entrance gates.

In the park, you can hear soothing bamboo flute music from loudspeakers with the latest generation of security cameras hanging next to them. A sign informs visitors that, in 2006, the National Committee for Quality Evaluation of Tourist Attractions gave the park an AAAA ranking, the second-highest grade. Hanging between elms and maple trees next to the pathway are thousands of plastic propellers sorted by color, turning in the wind. A food vendor is making lollipops out of light brown icing in the shape of the animals of the Chinese zodiac—dragons and horses are more expensive than rats and dogs. At the entrance to a ghost train there is a scary figure with a pig's head dressed in some sort of silk bathrobe. The highest point in the park is marked by a red pagoda—the emblem of Ürümqi—surrounded by the obligatory warning signs: "The garbage does not fall to the ground, the red mountain is more beautiful" and "Cherish your life no crossing."

Nothing in this park in the middle of Xinjiang province, even in the slightest way, hints at Uyghur traditions. Were it not for the conspicuous police presence, Hongshan could just as easily be in any other Chinese city.

I sit down on a wooden bench next to a small artificial pond about the size of a tennis court and around two feet deep. In the middle is a replica of an old water mill. A boy of about six or seven with an undercut hairstyle paddles a futuristic-looking plastic boat around the pond. Instead of oars, it has two bucket wheels on the sides that are operated by a hand crank. The possibilities are limited: he can go around the mill either clockwise or the other way; whatever the direction, it is still a circle.

The kid's grandma is standing beside the pond, watching and shouting at him to go right and not bump into anything. Then she looks at her cell, perhaps tapping in a few WeChat messages, maybe browsing for clothes on Taobao, possibly checking to see her latest rating on Sesame Credit. The boy notices that no one is watching him now, so he stops paddling and simply lets himself drift.

ACKNOWLEDGMENTS

Without the help of many kind people this book wouldn't have been possible. Five out of a possible five gratitude points to Joanna Szczepanska, Stefen Chow, Nora Reinhardt, Anastasiya Izhak, Haifen Nan, Lillian Zhang, Hallie Guo, Janine Borse, Tonia Sorrentino, Gilda Sahebi, Andreas Lorenz, Stefan Schultz, Antje Blinda, Anja Tiedge, Verena Töpper, Ruth Fend, Felicitas von Lovenberg, Bettina Feldweg, Verena Pritschow, Ulrike Ostermeyer, Petra Eggers, Christoph Rehage, Kai Strittmatter, Sébastien Lorandel, Luisa and Giorgio in Schilpario, Valentina in Bianzone, Traudl and Uli, and my parents.

Also huge *xiexie* to all Couchsurfing hosts who received me so warmly, as well as Binbin in Guangzhou, Jelena in Fenghuang, Kurt in Zhangjiajie, Fire in Beijing, Owen in Beijing, Yane in Tianjin, Jiannan and Tomas in Dalian, Taylor in Qingdao, Him in Xining, Yung Chung in Shanghai, Sunma in Shenzhen and Gus in Hong Kong.

NOTES

1. Ulf Meyer, "Shenzhen Stock Exchange," Arcspace, December 17, 2013, arcspace.com/feature/shenzhen-stock-exchange/.

2. Confucius, The Analects, trans. D.C. Lau (New York: Penguin Classics, 1979), 74.

3. Samuel Wade, "Minitrue: Don't Report on Kindergarten Abuse," China Digital Times, November 24, 2017, chinadigitaltimes.net/2017/11/minitrue-dont-report-comment-beijing-kindergarten-abuse/.

4. Samuel Wade, "Minitrue 2017: February—Smog, AI, HIV," China Digital Times, December 15, 2017, chinadigitaltimes.net/2017/12/minitrue-2017-february-smog-voice-recognition-hiv-infections/.

5. Josh Rudolph, "Minitrue: Delete News on Truck Drivers' Strike," China Digital Times, June 12, 2018, chinadigitaltimes.net/2018/06/minitrue-delete-news-on-truck-drivers-strike/.

6. Samuel Wade, "Minitrue: On U.S.–China Trade Tensions," China Digital Times, June 29, 2018, chinadigitaltimes.net/2018/06/minitrue-on-u-s-china-trade-tensions/.

7. Ibid.

8. Sophie Beach, "Minitrue: No Hyping North Korea Nuclear Test," China Digital Times, September 3, 2017, chinadigitaltimes.net/2017/09/minitrue-no-hyping-north-korea-nuclear-test/.

9. Samuel Wade, "Minitrue: 21 Rules on Coverage of the Two Sessions," *China Digital Times*, March 8, 2016, chinadigitaltimes.net/2016/03/minitrue-important-notices-coverage-two-sessions/.

10. Samuel Wade, "Minitrue: Defeat at the Tennis Table Tournament," *China Digital Times*, November 14, 2017, chinadigitaltimes.net/2017/11/minitrue-defeat-at-german-open-table-tennis-tournament/.

11. Josh Rudolph, "Minitrue: Follow Xinhua on Jiuzhaigou Earthquake," *China Digital Times*, August 8, 2017, chinadigitaltimes.net/2017/08/minitrue-follow-xinhuas-lead-jiuzhaigou-earthquake/.

12. Li Jing, "Go Big or Go Home: Guizhou Bets on 'Big Data,'" *Sixth Tone*, July 13, 2018, sixthtone.com/news/1002616/go-big-or-go-home-guizhou-bets-on-big-data.

13. Wang Wei, "The Bamboo Grove," trans. Jean Elizabeth Ward, All Poetry, accessed October 23, 2019, allpoetry.com/The-Bamboo-Grove.

14. Joseph Rock, "Konka Risumgongha: Holy Mountain of the Outlaws," *National Geographic*, July 1931, Volume 60, Number 1.

15. "Daocheng Yading Travel Guide and Tour Packages," Sichuan Travel Guide: More Than Pandas, accessed October 23, 2019, sichuantravelguide.com/daocheng-yading.html.

16. Rian Thum, "What Really Happens in China's 'Re-education' Camps," *New York Times*, May 15, 2018, nytimes.com/2018/05/15/opinion/china-re-education-camps.html.

17. "'Eradicating Ideological Viruses': China's Campaign of Repression against Xinjiang's Muslims," Human Rights Watch, September 9, 2018, hrw.org/report/2018/09/09/eradicating-ideological-viruses/chinas-campaign-repression-against-xinjiangs.